How We Made the WORLD a Better Place

How We Made the WORLD a Better Place

Kids and Teens Write on
How They Changed Their
Corner of the World

Compiled by the editors at Fairview Press

Fairview Press
MINNEAPOLIS

Published by Fairview Press, 2450 Riverside Avenue South, Minneapolis, MN 55454.

Library of Congress Cataloging-in-Publication Data

How we made the world a better place : kids and teens write on how
   they changed their corner of the world / compiled by the editors at
   Fairview Press
       p.   cm.
     ISBN 1-57749-079-7 (alk. paper)
       1. Child volunteers--United States--Case Studies.   2. Young
     volunteers--United States--Case Studies.   3. Helping behavior in
     children--United States--Case Studies.   I. Fairview Press.
     HQ784.V64H68   1998
     361.3'7'083--dc21   98-30153
                                                    CIP

First Printing: September 1998

Printed in the United States of America

02 01 00 99 98   7 6 5 4 3 2 1

Book cover: Cover Design by Laurie Duren

Interior design: Stanton Publications

Publisher's Note: Fairview Press publications, including *How We Made the World a Better Place*, do not necessarily reflect the philosophy of Fairview Health Services.

For a free current catalog of Fairview Press titles, please call toll-free 1-800-544-8207. Or visit our web site at www.Press.Fairview.org.

Contents

HEALING THE EARTH

Helping Those In Need

Companionship

Giving Is Better Than Receiving

FUND-RAISERS

ALCOHOL, TOBACCO, AND OTHER DRUGS

THE LARGER WORLD

COMMUNITY PRIDE

Foreword

I REMEMBER THE FIRST TIME I TOOK ACTION TO CHANGE THE world. I was twelve.

I was a child of the '60s and had trailed my older brother to enough rallies protesting the Vietnam War that I felt it was time to go one step further and make a real difference.

I sat down and composed a serious and forthright letter to President Lyndon Johnson asking—demanding—that he bring the American troops home from Vietnam.

To no one's surprise but my own, my efforts did not even result in a reply from President Johnson, much less an end to the war. I had changed nothing. Looking back, I think I had tackled too big a problem.

It took me years to discover what so many authors in this book already know—that it is the smaller actions that make the biggest difference.

In these stories, you will hear pride resonating in the words of young people who really have made a difference in the world—and were personally rewarded along the way. Each and every one of them found it within themselves to share kindness, motivate others, serve as a leader, and, many times, make a new lifelong friend.

You will smile as you read Amanda Dewey's "Small Acts," a touching story about saving baby ducks that had been rejected by their mother. In "Kids Helping Kids," you'll be inspired to hear how troubled youth with a history of behavior problems developed a program to teach younger kids to become good team players.

Think about what you can do in your own community as you hear from twelve-year-old Katie Crosbie, author of "Take Time to Make a Difference," who eloquently describes that, in the end, the most important things come from the heart.

Fifteen-year-old Emily Douglas didn't just get a letter from the president. As Sean Saffell describes in "Grandma's Gifts," Emily was invited to dinner with President Clinton. She won a national award for her volunteer work and got her photo in *Time Magazine*.

What Emily and all the other authors in this book have is a vision—and a willingness to work hard to accomplish their goals.

As you think about what you can do, take time to dream. As a Girl Scout Troop leader, a church schoolteacher, a parent, and a member of several boards, I have seen many dreams come true. This year, the girls in my Girl Scout Troop decided they wanted to give all the money they had raised in the last six years to an international cause. They considered making gift baskets to donate to refugee families resettling in America. But after further research, they became the official sponsor for a refugee family from Bosnia, whose homeland—indeed, whose own home—had been ripped apart by war.

The girls were at the airport as the family stepped off the plane, and they have helped the family every step of the way to build a new life in America. These girls have done something that most adults would never dare to try. Their vision and commitment led them to truly change the lives of these Bosnian refugees.

And this is what each of us can discover inside ourselves. There is hard work to be done, but the rewards are great. We may not all be able to stop a war or get a letter from the president, but as the authors of this book have demonstrated through their own compassion and dedication, each of us *can* change the world around us.

LINDSAY STRAND

Lindsay Strand is a former television reporter who has had some wonderful adventures with young people, including her own two children. She is convinced that the ideas of young people are every bit as good, and usually better, than those of adults.

Preface

IN OUR FAST-PACED WORLD OF BUSINESS AND TECHNOLOGY, WE often lose touch with other facets of life—the homeless, the elderly, the environment. Sometimes it takes a seven-year-old child to make us aware of the future of our planet. Such was the inspiration for the Fairview Press Publish-a-Story contest. We asked kids and teens across the country, "What have you done to make the world a better place?" The replies have been heartwarming, honest, and inspirational.

The winning essay, "Elsie," by Anna Evenson, is the story of an eleven-year-old girl who reluctantly takes a few minutes out of her day to visit an elderly neighbor. When she realizes how happy her neighbor is to see her, she can't help but keep coming back. Anna learns that it feels good to make someone else happy—and gains a lifelong friend in the process.

In "Take Time to Make a Difference," the second-place essay, twelve-year-old Katie Crosbie writes, "No, I haven't saved anyone's life, I haven't stopped a crisis in action, and I haven't yet discovered a cure for cancer. I have, however, offered to help people who looked like they needed help. I have smiled at people who looked dejected. I have stopped to talk with people who looked lonely." Katie's essay holds an important lesson for us all—that even the little things make a big difference in this world.

Third place goes to the Barbee siblings, Matt, Cheryl, and Karen, for their essay titled "Support Our Siblings." When Matt was diagnosed with several medical problems, he and his parents attended support groups, leaving Cheryl and Karen behind. The sisters realized that they needed support as well, so they formed their own group. SOS, a support group for kids on medication and their siblings, not only has had a profound impact on their community, but proves that people, both young and old, *can* help each other.

As more and more news headlines point to disillusioned youth caught in a net of apathy, we would do well to turn to those many kids and teens who have made positive contributions to our world. As these talented young writers have demonstrated, young people can and do make a difference. These writers offer hope for the future—for a healthier environment, a stronger community, and a heightened sense of sincerity. They underscore our belief that tomorrow's world is in good hands.

It is our hope that these essays will not only bring recognition to the young people who care so much about this world, but also spark a desire in others to make positive changes in the world around us. Let these young people be an inspiration to us all.

Fairview Press

Acknowledgments

Fairview Press would like to thank the following organizations for their gracious support of this project. Without them, this book would not have been possible.

For their sponsorship, financial and otherwise, we would like to thank:

Automated Mailing Corporation
Capital City Pride
Cold Side Silkscreening
DRAGnet
Fairview Foundation
Hungry Mind Bookstore
Mall of America
Message! Products
Minnesota Vikings
Simek's
Soderberg Florist
Stanton Publications
SuperAmerica
Tiro Industries
Walgreens

For her special contribution to this project, we sincerely thank Lindsay Strand.

We would also like to thank our panel of judges, whose time and effort have contributed so much to this book:

Professor Chester G. Anderson, University of Minnesota
Mayor Sharon Sayles Belton of Minneapolis
John Burstein, also known as Slim Goodbody
Marly Cornell, Fairview Health Services
Laurie Beth Fitz, American Cancer Society
Senator Rod Grams of Minnesota
Nkauj'lis Lyfoung, KTCA's *Don't Believe the Hype*
Patrice Snead, Minnesota History Center

Finally, for the heart behind the book and the words within each story, we would like to thank all of the kids and teens who sent in their essays. Though the final choices for publication were difficult, every essay we received contributed to this remarkable book—and to a better world. Thank you all, from Fairview Press.

KIDS HELPING KIDS

Kids Helping Kids

....

Chris, age 13; Quantay, age 11; Ricky, age 9;
Matt, age 12; Tyreese, age 12; William, age 12;
Ralph, age 12; and Jeremy, age 13

IT ALL BEGAN ABOUT A YEAR AND A HALF AGO. OUR TEACHER decided it would be a good experience for us to help younger students at another school. You see, we don't go to a regular public school. We attend school at the children's residential facility where we live. There are fourteen other schools like ours in the country, and our teacher picked one with younger students for us to visit. This is how we began helping younger kids.

Our class consists of eight guys, ranging in age from nine to thirteen. We are all here because we've been in some kind of trouble, but we're trying to change. It's hard, but as they say, it takes a bigger man to change his way than to not change at all.

Every Thursday, we get together with the kids and work on different behaviors. We teach them how to share, play games fairly, follow the rules in sports, and be good team players. We also work with them on math, reading, art, and computer skills. We try to be good role models for the younger children, showing them how to be responsible and act appropriately.

We are not only there to help these kids, we are also their friends. It is difficult for many of them to trust anyone because of what has happened to them in the past. We know how they feel, so we try to be there for them, giving them someone to look up to and lean on. We build our own self-esteem while we help them build theirs. We enjoy helping these kids. It makes us feel good.

The children are special to us. We really love them and enjoy being around them. We hope that after we move on from this program, the next group will keep the tradition going.

Twelve Years and Counting

....

Erin Banholzer, age 12

I HELPED TO MAKE THE WORLD A BETTER PLACE WHEN MY Girl Scout troop helped younger girls learn the proper way to set up a campsite quickly and safely.

While the two troops drove to camp, everyone was nervous because we didn't know each other. When we arrived, there was lots of work to be done. It was cold, so we first taught the girls how to set up camp and get a fire going. They were all fascinated by the fire and understood the lessons about safety. Then, each older girl took a group of younger girls and taught them one basic chore. I taught my group how to light and clean a lantern. Some of the other Scouts taught the little girls how to tie knots or how to clean out a cabin. Some even got the privilege of learning how to clean the latrine!

After we had taught them the basic skills, my group did a skit to present our information to the other groups. Almost everyone did a skit of some kind. When each group was done, we had snack mix and hot chocolate. Finally, we played games like Telephone until it was time to go home.

The girls still haven't gone on a camping trip on their own, but when they do, they will be ready. And I am glad I could help. On our first try, it took our group three hours to set up camp. Now it only takes thirty minutes.

On Patrol

....

Alex Rick, age 12

IN MY ELEMENTARY SCHOOL, WE HAD A GROUP OF STUDENTS who were chosen by teachers to be on the safety patrol. This story is about my experiences.

One school day, I got a letter that said I would be on safety patrol the next year. I was so happy, because I looked up to the kids on the safety patrol. I thought they were cool, and now I was going to be one of them. What made it even more fun was that some of my friends were going to be patrols, also.

We couldn't wait until next year. That summer we each got letters that said we were supposed to go to the school and have our first patrol meeting. The day of the meeting, I was at my friend Pat's house. So when the time came, we rode our bikes to school and waited for the other people to get there. When they did, we strolled into the classroom where the meeting was to take place. When everyone got there, my teacher and the head of the patrols, Mr. Mulroy, started the meeting. After the meeting, Pat and I went back to his house and played with our new badges.

On the first day of fifth grade, my fellow patrols and I started our duties. My first job was to tell everyone in school which buses had arrived. I got to use the school intercom! Even though I got in trouble for goofing around, it was still fun. Sometimes, if the person gave me the wrong buses, I got in trouble.

Every month or so, we switched jobs. On some of the coldest days in winter, I was outside helping kids cross the streets. In the spring, when I had that job again, I stepped out and put my flag down so the kids could cross the street, and a car almost ran me over.

Being a patrol had its ups and downs. A few of us got to go to Valley Fair, and we sometimes got hot cocoa from the cooks on really cold days. The downs included being outside on frigid winter days and getting blamed for other people messing up. Still, it was fun helping other kids cross the streets, getting them to their buses, and doing jobs like that. Helping other people makes me feel good.

Books Get Waterlogged, Girl Scouts to the Rescue!

....

Taylor R. Kopacka, age 11;
Ryann M. Kopacka, age 9; and
Karin K. Singler, age 11

OUR GIRL SCOUT TROOP 2216 STARTED THINKING ABOUT OUR project in 1997, when spring floods were raging in North Dakota. Our assistant leader, who used to live in North Dakota, heard from a friend that an elementary school would open in the fall without a school library. Our troop decided to collect books for the school. We collected over three thousand books for the Lewis and Clark Elementary School in Grand Forks, North Dakota.

We put out flyers all over our neighborhood and other neighborhoods in the area. We also put an article in the newspaper asking people to donate books that their children had outgrown. We put similar articles in Lake Windward Elementary School's *Gator Gram* and *Great Gator Paper*, as well as Findley Oaks' *Findley Flyer*. We told them that some of the Girl Scouts would be collecting books at the Windward Pool parking lot.

We decided to send a camera with the books we collected, so that Lewis and Clark could take pictures of their school and the new library. We sent the camera with the Sather truck driver. Sather Trucking Company donated the shipping of all our books.

The first day of book collecting was not so hot. We had put out hundreds of flyers the day before, and we were hoping people would give at least one book to the cause. In most neighborhoods, no one gave us any books. We went to the pool parking lot to wait and see if anybody showed up. We were lucky. We got a few books.

At our Scout meeting, we talked about our collection effort and decided we weren't going to give up. Those kids in Grand Forks needed books.

Over the next week, we asked a private elementary school, two middle schools, and two high schools if any of their students would like to donate books. Talk about a lot of books! The private school gave the biggest donation. We went to more neighborhoods and collected more and more books. Our own school even donated an entire set of encyclopedias.

After that week, we counted over three thousand books! We felt mighty pleased with ourselves and wished we could read many of the books we had collected. When packing and shipping day came, we wondered if the school in North Dakota would like all the books we had collected. We couldn't wait to hear from them and see the pictures they would take.

When the books got to the Lewis and Clark Elementary School, the principal called us. He was amazed at how many books our troop had collected. We had gathered enough books to double their library.

The principal took pictures of the delivery truck with the books being unloaded, the school, the new library, and the Girl Scout troop that helped catalog and put away the books. They sent us the pictures, along with gracious notes from the librarian to each of us. We read them at our next Girl Scout meeting. When the project was over, we felt that we made a difference to a fellow community—kids just like us!

Peer Mediation Helps

....

Willie Ruckel, age 11

I HAVE DONE MANY GREAT THINGS IN MY LIFE. ONE OF THEM IS Peer Mediation, a five-step process that helps people solve their problems.

To my surprise, I was elected by my fourth-grade class. I was sure my class was going to pick someone else. I had to go to many training sessions to learn how to become a peer mediator, but I learned a lot not only about Peer Mediation but also things I could use on the long road of life.

Peer Mediation works like this. Two or more people, called disputants, contact the office and set a date for mediation. When that date arrives, another peer mediator and I come in to help the disputants solve their problems by using the five-step process. We usually pull it off. If the mediation does not work, we set up another date—this time with an adult—or, if the disputants choose to stop the process, we do no more.

It is a pleasure helping people solve their problems. The feeling inside is great. We help with problems ranging from name-calling to extreme anger. If a problem involves weapons, harassment, drugs, or other terrible problems, we are not allowed to mediate.

It is difficult to mediate, but I feel that I have been successful. To me, it is one of the best things to do. I am glad I can help other people.

Hot Masks, Cool Dreams

....

Kate Zabbia, age 16

I COULD BARELY SEE. A SPONGE-LIKE, SMALL-NETTED WEBBING covered almost all of my vision. It was extremely hot, and my long bangs were stuck to my cheeks, but I couldn't reach up to brush them off my face. If I did, the children would be able to see who was inside the mask. Miserable and uncomfortable, I tried to recall what made me participate in this project in the first place.

Tonight was the night of the annual Tucker Elementary Literacy Night, when the first- and second-grade students could show parents their classroom and learn at the same time. My high school Key Club was helping out by serving food, assisting families, and dressing up like storybook characters.

Joe, the club president, insisted a few days before that I be the one to dress up in a costume. I thought it could be fun, so I showed up to see what it was all about. Ms. Tricou, the school librarian, guided Mark, Brittany, Shane, and me down the hallway to give us our new identities. There, she opened four boxes and held up a different costume for each of us. Brittany immediately wanted Curious George. Mark saw the head of his costume and fell in love with Lyle the Crocodile, while Shane happily took Clifford. Since I was the last female, I took Madeline, a storybook orphan.

The good thing about my outfit was that I didn't have a full body suit. Mark, Brittany, and Shane had one-piece costumes with sleeves and pants. I had only a large navy cloak that extended past my knees, showing my Nike sneakers. I didn't have to wear gloves, either.

Once the four of us got used to the huge masks, Ms. Tricou walked us across the street to the school. Our instructions were to greet the kids, take pictures with them, and just wave. Talking was permitted but not recommended.

We were greeted in the main room with wide eyes and smiles. More kids were fascinated with Clifford and Curious George, but Mark and I didn't mind. Walking around with such heavy head-pieces, it was hard to get used to our costumes. The glare of the sun in the window knocked all four of us off balance, so Joe guided us into the cafeteria where most of the action was taking place.

Children were everywhere. There were tables lined up on the sides of the cafeteria, with teachers at each assisting in a fun learning session. Our duty as storybook characters was obvious when we entered the cafeteria doors. Children began pointing and waving as soon as they saw us.

As we walked around, I began to get hot, which meant Mark, Shane, and Brittany must have been burning up. Even though it was pulled back in a ponytail, my hair was falling on my chin, annoying me. But I couldn't reach my hand under the chin of my mask—it wouldn't look realistic anymore. I wouldn't look like the real Madeline.

As I watched Joe running around, trying to keep things organized, I felt jealous that he was free, in loose clothes, enjoying the cool air conditioner. Then, I felt a tap on the back of my coat. I turned to see a large-eyed, very small girl peering up at me.

"Hi," she said shyly. Her voice was so faint that I could barely hear her under my costume. She waved, then ran off.

I don't know why, but it was her small greeting that inspired me to keep going in my heavy disguise the rest of the night. I could tell that the awe and fascination of children kept my other three friends from dismantling their stuffy costumes as well. The eyes of each child were like an adhesive, pulling the four of us back into our roles, keeping us from throwing off our uncomfortable costumes to run away free. The young children were captivated by our presence. Here we were, their favorite storybook characters, alive and walking around among them. Though many children knew we weren't actually the real characters, they still got a kick out of meeting us and shaking our hands.

When Joe checked on us later in the evening, I realized I didn't envy him anymore. He didn't get giant hugs from children half his size or a high five from a seven-year-old. He wasn't invited to pose for a picture with three little girls standing beside him. Even though there was a mask obstructing my view, wisps of hair in my eyes and stuck to my face, and a hot, heavy cape weighing down my body, nothing could bring me down from the wonderful feeling I had at that moment.

Support Our Siblings

....

The Barbee Siblings: Matt, age 13;
Cheryl, age 12; and Karen, age 8

To help our community be a better place, we created a support group for the brothers and sisters of children who are on medication. We chose this project because our brother has had multiple medical problems throughout his childhood, including A.D.H.D., obsessive-compulsive behaviors, tons of allergies, and, most recently, Asperger's Syndrome.

Our brother and our parents have support groups they can attend. But when the three of them leave for their sessions, we are always left behind. From early childhood, we remember feeling left out, almost excluded. As siblings, we need to understand not only how our brother's illnesses and disorders affect our parents and brother, but how they affect us. We know that talking with others who are in a similar situation helps. Our parents and brother need the support they get from others. So do we.

Support Our Siblings (SOS) was the result. To find a place to hold our meetings, Karen made an appointment with Mr. Dallolio, our school counselor, and Mr. Cunningham, the school principal. We had no idea they would be so enthusiastic about it. We chose the school library for our meeting place, refined our plans for the group, and set a date for the first meeting. SOS would be open to kids ages eight to fourteen. We advertised the meeting by sending flyers to nearby schools.

It was surprising how fast our idea bloomed. Everyone we contacted was supportive. Catlin Printing donated 1,500 color copies for the flyers. Mr. Dallolio helped us find volunteer counselors, while Mr. Cunningham supplied refreshments. We thought it would be fun to wrap up the evening with pizza for everyone, and the manager from the local Domino's donated to our cause. Albertson's, a local supermarket, contributed salad, soda, and paper plates. Saint Alphonsus Hospital donated $100, which we used to buy thank-you gifts for the counselors who volunteered their time.

A journalist from our local newspaper came to interview the three of us at our house when he heard about our idea. His article started our phone ringing with people wanting to register. By the afternoon of March 31, fifty-five people had registered for the first SOS meeting.

We arrived at the school at 4:00 P.M. to set up. We put out name tags, set up the cafeteria for our pizza dinner, and put hand-made signs throughout the school to direct people to the meeting place in the library. Everything went smoothly until about 4:55, when fifteen unregistered people showed up. It was hectic trying to make new name tags, figure out which groups to put the new people in, and start the meeting on time!

At the start of the meeting, we greeted everyone and thanked the businesses that had donated food or money. Then we introduced our brother, Matt, who was the inspiration for SOS. Meanwhile, Mom slipped out to call Domino's. We needed more pizza for the fifteen additional people.

We showed a movie about dealing with stress in families, from a kid's perspective, then we broke into small discussion groups with one counselor per group. At the end of the hour, we gave the counselors a plant and two free movie tickets. The entire group enjoyed the donated pizza, salad, chips, pop, and ice cream, and we passed out paper and pencils for participants to write down the names and phone numbers of friends they had made, so they could call each other when they needed someone to talk to.

Overall, we were very pleased with our SOS night. (If we had it to do over, we would make preregistration a must to eliminate the last-minute rush.) Afterward, we published a thank-you note in our local newspaper to all those who helped make our first SOS meeting a success. We couldn't have done it alone. We also wanted to tell the public that we were planning another meeting in the fall.

We all need to know we are not alone. Many families experience the same frustrations and difficulties. Somehow it helps knowing we're not the only ones struggling. We can make a difference in our community by supporting each other. We can help each other. And we did!

THE LITTLE THINGS

Together We Can Do So Much

Chelsey Hannah, age 12

THE WORLD AROUND US IS THE MOST MAGNIFICENT THING EVER created. It has been here for billions of years, providing life for many wondrous beings. There are problems on this planet, but they are problems that can be fixed. With the help of everyone, the bumps on the road will be smoothed out, and the world will become a better place.

I have done my part by caring for small children, for my peers, for the elderly, for the environment. Last year, I was a member of the student council. We all worked hard collecting pennies to give to victims of leukemia. A lot of money was raised, and I know we all felt good inside knowing that it could help save someone's life.

When I was in Girl Scouts, we also did a lot of things to help and care for people. Most memorable was singing Christmas carols to people in town homes. They all had a delightful look of joy on their faces.

My love for children persuaded me to beg my parents to let me help in our church nursery. When they finally agreed, I was thrilled. Working almost every week, I got to know the children, their parents, and the other supervisors. All were very kind, and we shared many happy times together.

One person's trash can become another person's treasure. In third grade, with that saying in mind, each person in my class constructed a bird out of an old light bulb. Mine was a hummingbird. Recycling in this way helps prevent the overuse of landfills. That same year, my class went on a field trip to a local park to pick up litter. Some people aren't as kind to the environment as others. We spent an entire day cleaning up the park and caring for a large grove of trees.

As children grow older, schoolwork gets harder. Some students struggle to understand their work. To help those students who would like to improve their grades, I'm involved in a program at my school called Peer Tutoring. The other tutors and I meet with students once or twice a week to help them understand their work. I also help my peers by helping them sort out their problems. Everyone is different, and sometimes those differences cause conflicts. In a program called Peer Mediation, I try to help my peers resolve their problems.

Elderly people who live alone sometimes need help putting a smile on their face around the holidays. This year, some of my classes have been busily decorating bags for my English teacher. She puts treats in them and gives them to the elderly. Special gifts like these always bring a little bit of happiness into a lonely person's life.

I care about all people and hope that I have made a difference in someone's life. Although I alone can do so little, if every person does something small, together we can do so much.

People Helping People

....

Zachary Potts, age 12

THE WORLD IS A WONDERFUL PLACE, AND IT IS NOTHING TO be wasted.

Hi, my name is Zack Potts. I've done a lot of things to make the world a better place, but I'd have to say that collecting food for the food shelf was the most fun. I did it for Cub Scouts and we went all around Andover collecting. My friends and I collected over one-hundred pounds of food.

I also tried to help other kids when some of the kids in my fourth-grade class and I went to talk to some first-grade kids about school. We talked about how they're going to have to do well in school and the problems they might face.

When a bad storm came last summer, the damage was horrible. There were a whole bunch of trees down, houses damaged, cars damaged. It was unbelievable. But the neighborhood came together and helped fix everything.

Even though all the things I told you about are good things to do, I think there is nothing better than being a good person. I think I'm a good person because I'm kind and generous and I'll help anybody who needs help.

There are a lot of good people in this world, and that is the way it should be.

Take Time to Make a Difference

Katie Crosbie, age 12

MAYBE IT'S THE LITTLE, UNEXPECTED THINGS THAT COUNT THE most—smiling at a lonely person in a store, holding the door for a stranger, saying hello to someone who isn't your friend, asking someone to join you for lunch, or complimenting an acquaintance on the way he or she looks or for a job well done.

Of the things I have done that have made a difference to others, the most important things may not seem all that noteworthy. For example, simply getting involved in school, church, and community activities makes a difference to a lot of people. When I perform in a play, sing in a choir, or volunteer for a charitable cause, I know I have made a difference when I see the warm expressions on people's faces.

The most important things I can give are the things that come from my heart. Taking time to care about others, not always putting myself first, makes a big difference.

Have you ever noticed how an attitude is contagious? If someone is cheerful and friendly, it's likely that others will be friendlier, too. I try to make a difference by being friendly to everyone, not just my closest friends. People often expect a card on their birthday, but think of the difference it would make to your grandma or grandpa if you sent them a letter for no reason, just to make their trip to the mailbox worthwhile.

No, I haven't saved anyone's life, I haven't stopped a crisis in action, and I haven't yet discovered a cure for cancer. I have, however, offered to help people who looked like they needed help. I have smiled at people who looked dejected. I have stopped to talk with people who looked lonely. I have set a good example for younger people in my community. And, I have given my time and talent to the church, my school, and my community.

These things—the little things—make the world a better place. And I plan to continue making a difference in the world I am so proud to be part of!

If I Could Change the World

Kyle Benkofske, age 12

....

I HAVE DONE MANY IMPORTANT THINGS IN MY LIFE. THESE things have been big and small, but no matter how small, these deeds have all helped make the world a better place.

The most important thing I did was helping out with my baby cousin, Connor. Connor had leukemia, a type of cancer. Most of my spare weekends were spent with him watching *Barney*. He loved that show. After two years of fighting his disease, he died. Connor was brain dead and his kidneys had failed him. His parents decided to turn off the machines that were keeping him alive. There is no way I will ever forget those precious moments with him. When I grow up, I hope to go to college to be a doctor so I can help people like Connor. No one should have to go through so much pain because of a disease.

Another thing I do is visit my great-grandma at her nursing home in Milbank, South Dakota. She hasn't been doing so well. She is in her eighties now. I wish she could live forever. When I visit her, I fill her in on all the things that have happened to me since my last visit. She really likes it when I visit. I like our visits, too. Before she moved into the nursing home, I used to do work in her garden. It was hard work, but I loved it.

In my life, helping out my grandpa is very important to me. Sometimes I mow his lawn when he doesn't feel good. I think it is a lot of fun. It only takes about an hour, but it still helps him out a lot.

I think that helping people should always come first. But I also do things for the earth. I only hope my deeds will influence you to also help make the world a better place.

I recall when my family and I planted a ton of baby pine trees. In the summer, I water them all the time. Also, in my house I am the garbage man. I have a big family and we usually have a lot of garbage. So I try to minimize it by recycling. Recycling takes away a lot of garbage, and I suggest that everyone recycle to lessen the amount of garbage in the world.

All That I Can Do

....

Joseph P. Wilson, age 12

EVEN THOUGH IT MAY NOT SEEM LIKE A BIG DEAL, I TRY TO HELP out the world as much as I can.

I can recall a time a couple of years ago when I decided our family should start recycling. Before, we would just throw away pop cans and newspaper. I brought the topic up to my parents, and, with hardly any effort at all, I persuaded them to hop on the bandwagon and start recycling.

Another thing that sticks in my mind happened back in first grade when I won a drawing contest. At the time, my class was raising money to put into a fund to help take care of an animal in the zoo. After thinking about it overnight, I decided to put my $50 winnings toward the fund. That was one of the nicest things I've ever done.

Mediation is another thing I do to help. Last week, I was called upon to mediate. Doing this makes me feel as if I'm making a difference in someone's life by helping to solve a problem.

Like many kids my age, I go to confirmation classes. My class does community service. I remember one time in particular because it happened recently. Five other people and I headed over to a man's house to help him pack boxes to send to the Salvation Army. It was cold, but, after an hour of boxing and taping, we stood back and admired a full driveway of packed boxes.

If We Work Together We Can Make It Better

Kelsy M. Lane, age 11

I HAVEN'T DONE ANYTHING SPECIAL OR GREAT TO MAKE THE world a better place, but I have done a few things here and there that have helped.

When I was in second grade, my dad worked in a building with a pop machine. I had been collecting pop tops for the Ronald McDonald house for a long time, so I thought this was a good opportunity to get some pop tops. My dad and I put an envelope for the pop tops on the side of the pop machine, and when the envelope got full I would bring the pop tops to school with me.

When I was in third grade, my teacher brought in UNICEF boxes. She told us to go door to door on Halloween and ask people to please give some money to the cause. I got scared because I was very shy. The first few times I only said, "Trick or treat." My friend's brother asked people for a while, and then I tried again. All together, I made $12!

On Earth Day, when I was nine, my friend's little brother and I went around his neighborhood and picked up trash. We weren't even all the way around the block when our garbage bags were full!

I can think of so many little things that I can do to make the world a better place, I am going to try to do a lot more.

The Little Things
That Count

....

Stacy Jorgenson, age 11

HAVE YOU EVER HAD THAT FEELING IN YOUR STOMACH WHEN you know you did something to help somebody? Even small things can save this world.

I was in Girl Scouts for about four years. We did a lot of fun activities, but we also did community service work. Occasionally we would go to the Elk's Club to help serve dinner to the elderly and disabled. This was one of the hardest community service projects we did because the dinners were held in a small, smoky area. During the holidays, we would decorate cards and place mats that were delivered through the Meals on Wheels program.

My Girl Scout troop also adopted two parks. It was our responsibility to keep the litter picked up and the ground raked.

Near Christmastime, my troop would go caroling around different neighborhoods. It got really cold outside, but I wanted to make people feel happy and cheerful! Once we went to a nursing home to sing Christmas carols. I had a fun time doing this. It made me feel good to know I was making people feel happy.

A short time after Halloween, my troop went to people's houses and handed out bags for a food drive. About a week later, we picked up the bags full of food and gave them to a charity.

Just recently a girl from Fred Moore, a school close to mine, got hit by a car and was killed. My English class and I made sympathy cards for her family. It made us feel good knowing we could help them through such a hard time.

Baby-sitting may not seem like a hard job, but when you baby-sit two little kids, it can be tough! To help out, my best friend and I would usually baby-sit her younger brother and sister—for free. It was fun once I got to know the kids. And we were really making a difference.

These things, the little things, do help to make the world a nicer place to be. Each and every act of kindness counts.

Good Deeds

Cassi Lea Ulrich, age 12

MY FAMILY AND I BELIEVE THAT GIVING IS BETTER THAN RE-ceiving. I have helped many different people and places in my lifetime.

I really like to help charitable causes. My family and I rode in the MS-30, a thirty-mile bike ride to help find a cure for Multiple Sclerosis. My grandma has MS, and we want her to get better. Also, when my clothes get too small for me, I donate them to the Epilepsy Foundation and the Goodwill. And I always bring in food for school. We have bag day, box day, and can day. We do this for people who don't have enough money to buy their own food.

I also feel strongly about the environment. Every summer, my friend Mallory and I pick up litter on our hill. The hill is about 660 feet long, which is one-eighth of a mile. After we pick up all the litter—and sometimes there's a lot of it—we go over to the neighbors. They usually have a treat for us. We do not pick up litter for a prize or for money; we do it for the satisfaction of a clean environment.

My family and I feel strongly about making and keeping our world clean. Whenever we go camping, we never litter. We either burn our trash or throw it away. We like to camp in a clean campground.

There are lots of ways to make the world a better place. For my part, I like what I do for the world I live in.

There's No Such Thing as Too Much

·····································

Paula Johnson, age 12

THROUGHOUT MY LIFE, I'VE DONE MANY THINGS FOR THE world and the environment. Even though the things I do don't seem like a lot to me, if everyone did these things the world would be a better place.

I contribute to many different organizations, such as Toys for Tots, Goodwill, Adopt-a-Family, the Salvation Army, Santa Anonymous, local food shelves, and many others. The reason I give to all these places is because it makes me feel good to know that my gifts really mean a lot to someone else. Perhaps I could be saving someone's life with each gift.

I've done many things to help my elders as well. For example, in school we decorate bags for the holidays to give the elderly treats and meals. My school also made cards for a family whose daughter had been hit by a car. She was hit while walking home from school with a friend. A couple of days later, she died.

I do things outside of school as well. My sister, the neighbor kids, and I go caroling to houses around Christmastime. In the spring, summer, and fall, I mow the lawn for my parents. I don't use the riding mower, though, just the pusher. Most people think mowing the lawn is hard and boring. I think the exact opposite; it's fun and easy.

I believe helping peers and younger children is important. I especially enjoy helping younger children because they ask so many questions. My giving them an answer could help them later in life. But I try to help my peers, too. When someone new came to our school and didn't have any friends, my friends and I asked her to sit with us. Being nice to someone is very important and makes a good example for others.

Finally, I encourage everyone I know to stop smoking, or not to start in the first place. Smoking is very dangerous. It can cause cancer and other diseases, as well as bad breath and wrinkles early in life. It's also bad for the environment and other people. Smoke from others is sometimes worse than smoking yourself.

I think people should do more to help everyone. I do these things because it makes me feel good, and you should too—not to fit in or because someone is making you, but because it's the right thing to do and you want to. Life's a privilege and should be lived to the fullest. Do everything you can today, so you never have to look back and say, "I wish I had done this," or "I should have done that." Instead, at the end of your life you can be proud of yourself and what you have accomplished. Remember, you can never do too much!

HEALING THE EARTH

A Better World

....

Courtney Casperson, age 7

I PLANT FLOWERS IN THE SPRING AND SUMMER BECAUSE THEY are pretty and they smell pretty. I like the plants and I like the beauty in nature. I like nature, and you should like it, too.

We should all plant flowers and trees to make a better world.

C.A.R.E.

....

Children Accepting Responsibility for the Earth
5th Grade, Room 45, El Verano Elementary School

HELLO. WE ARE A GROUP OF FIFTH GRADERS ON A QUEST. A quest to help heal our earth. We know that we need to help if our own children are to have all that we have. Someone has to set the pace, and we are trying our best to do all that we can. We care a lot about the environment. We call ourselves C.A.R.E., which stands for Children Accepting Responsibility for the Earth. We are on a quest to be involved and to get others involved, too. We've designed and made magnets for cars that say "One Earth . . . One People . . . One Chance . . ." and "Think Environmentally."

Our logo, a picture of three children hugging the earth, represents how everyone needs to care. Many children do care and will try to make a difference by doing whatever they can.

We have many goals this year. Our main goal is to spread the word. We designed and wrote the car magnets as well as a brochure—and we paid for them with our own hard-earned money. We collected aluminum cans all over town, we recycled aluminum from window screens that we dismantled, and we are selling environmentally-themed T-shirts to raise money. We also received some donations and community support. We really want our local community to become environmentally aware.

Another goal is to keep up with many established programs at El Verano Elementary School: the comprehensive recycling program, Point Reyes fire restoration work, and environmental living experiences at the Clem Miller Education Center at Point Reyes

National Seashore. We also continue to work at the Van Hoosear Wildflower Preserve, planting wildflowers and starting trees from seed to transplant later in the year.

We've also started a massive letter-writing campaign. We have written to the President, the Governor of California, the entire Senate Committee on the Environment and Public Works, the House Committee on Resources, and every single political office we felt might help make a difference environmentally. We have also written letters to all 100 Senators and 435 Representatives in the House asking for help in getting this country to think more environmentally and asking them to think about Senate Bill 1180, which we learned from our research may weaken the Endangered Species Recovery Act. We purchased all the stamps for these letters with our own money, and most of the envelopes were recycled from a card company that throws out envelopes that have no card.

We have taken an interest in the Endangered Species Recovery Act because we have adopted a few endangered animals with our money already. We adopted an adult cheetah, a humpback whale named Olympia—named for the scars on her side that are in the shape of the Olympic symbol—and two manatees, Howie and Flash. When we started writing to the Save the Manatee Club, we found out that the club was taking care of nineteen other endangered manatees. We were so taken by each manatee's picture and story that we decided to raise enough money to adopt all nineteen, not including the two we'd already adopted. In all, we have now adopted twenty-four endangered animals.

Another goal we have involves wood ducks in California. Over the summer, our class helped Atwood Ranch release eighteen baby California wood ducks in newly restored Calabasas Creek. We now plan to provide and install the nesting boxes necessary for these ducks to survive. Our class will be in charge of monitoring the boxes and the ducks, including their survival in the area. One of the dangers these ducks face comes from the bass in a nearby lake. Bass prey on baby ducks.

Our class was asked to provide a list of ways to change the environment. This and other real-life experience is the type children need, the type we will never forget. Real-life experiences mean real problems that students can help solve.

Staying with our original quest to promote environmental awareness in our school and community, we're also organizing creek clean-ups at Maxwell Park for many classes. As soon as possible, we will take along a second-grade "buddy class." We have to spread the word by having other children be involved and committed.

As you can see, we are very busy putting our time into helping the environment. We work hard, but love it. It may be hard to believe, but the work doesn't seem so bad when you know you're doing something your community and the entire world will benefit from. We know something must be done. We're hoping others will get excited and want to help, too! Like a student in our class said, "It's not like we can use this earth up and just go pick a new earth . . . like picking a new apple when the one you have is rotten."

Forest of Memories

....

Bryce Haugen, age 12

THE SMELL OF PINE AND CEDAR TREES WAS IN THE SPRING air. The beautiful flowers, with their morning dew, sparkled in the sunlight.

This is what the third grade classes at Andover Elementary School had planted the previous year. I looked at the pine tree I had helped plant and thought about what a gigantic tree the young pine would grow up to be. This forest was a great treasure to our school. I don't know one student who helped create it who wasn't extremely proud. In this small forest, we planted things like oak, pine, and cedar trees, and in the garden, we planted various flowers.

Mr. Zumberge, my third-grade teacher, was probably the teacher who had the greatest influence on me. He encouraged me to excel both academically and in the real world. With his help, we created a wonderful haven for pupils to relax in during recess. Creating this small forest also provided a wonderful opportunity for me and other students to change the environment in a good way, and to boost our self-esteem. I cannot describe the gratification I felt after helping to plant this beautiful forest. It was one of the greatest emotions a person could ever experience.

Helping to build or improve an area is an easy way to increase the happiness of others. It creates a sense of accomplishment. And by helping out with the forest and garden, students like myself built a reputation with the community as caring people. Now, as I walk through these woods, I am reminded of many magnificent memories of third grade—memories I will cherish for a lifetime.

Kids for Saving the Earth

....

Bethany Ann King, age 12

IN ELEMENTARY SCHOOL, I WAS PART OF A SCHOOL ORGANIZA-tion called Kids for Saving the Earth (KSE). I had been part of the club for three years last year, when I decided to run for vice president of the club.

Running for election took a lot of work. I had to give a speech and everything! Luckily, I was only running against one other person. On the day of the election, I gave a short speech. I must have done okay because four days later I found out I was the new vice president. As vice president, I had almost the same responsi-bilities as the president. I was required to take responsibility for club meetings, club money, and field trips. And, if the president was absent, I would take over.

KSE is all about kids taking care of the world we live in and learning more about it, too. We did a lot of cooperative learning with the Columbus Zoo. We went there a couple of times, and sometimes they came to our school. We learned a lot about ani-mals, pollution, and recycling. We also voted on animals to adopt, such as endangered animals like the Emu.

We had to have a lot of money to adopt the larger animals, so we held fund-raisers like spaghetti dinners. We were usually able to raise $800 to $1,000 with each spaghetti dinner, and we used the money to adopt many animals at the same time. We also used some of the money for field trips.

My favorite field trip was when we went to the recycling center. We learned about the importance of recycling, and that it takes newspapers almost ten years to disintegrate! Sometimes we would go out in the wooded area around the school and put up bird feeders made with pinecones and peanut butter; sometimes we just picked up trash. We also had a special garden, called the Granby Garden, where we planted vegetables. Sometimes we sent them to the Franklin County Fair where we received blue ribbons.

I am glad I decided to be a member of such a neat club where peers got an opportunity to work together. We helped make a real difference. We also learned about being peaceful and helpful where we live.

I wish my school now offered a club like KSE. It could offer students a way to feel like they could make a difference in their environment. We do participate in Worthington Service Day, but wouldn't it be great to have the opportunity to make a contribution all year long?

When I Am Old Enough

....

Ian L. Hagen, age 7

I AM STILL YOUNG, BUT I ALREADY HAVE PLANS TO HELP MAKE A better world when I am old enough. I will never litter or throw other things on the ground. If there is any garbage on the ground, I will pick up every last bit of it. If there are beer cans on the ground, I will pick them up and bring them to my mom and dad. By doing these things, I will help make the world a better place.

One Little Area on This Earth

Vy T. Trinh, age 13

I'M ONLY A SEVENTH GRADER AT PERRY MIDDLE SCHOOL, BUT already in my life I have helped make the world a better place. It was during fourth grade, but I remember it as if it were yesterday. I helped with my school, Bluffsview Elementary, to pick up trash on the school's property.

The land wasn't just for students who attended our school. It was also for the neighborhood. People went walking in the mornings on our blacktop, they would also walk their pets. Baseball games were held on the baseball diamond and soccer games were held on the grassy fields around the school. Children played on both the playground and the basketball courts. The kindergarten area was where my sister played at recess during that school year.

We had a contest with eighteen other classes, from first grade through sixth, to see which class could pick up the most trash. Each class was to go outside separately for ten to fifteen minutes to collect as much trash as they could. Each class was sent out by grade, starting with the lowest grade level. My grade was stuck smack in the middle, meaning we had to wait our turn. I couldn't wait to begin. I love competition.

When it was finally my class's turn, I thought, "We won't find that much trash. Everyone else probably took most of it. We will probably lose." But I was wrong. There was lots of trash left, despite so many other classes going before ours. I guess I never really noticed how dirty the school grounds were until that day. Trash was everywhere—under the mulch, in the grass, on the blacktop, around the basketball court, even on the baseball diamond.

We collected a lot. Some boys in our class found two huge pieces of cardboard, plus we managed to fill two big black trash bags. During our trash hunt, the principal came out to watch. She told us we had collected a lot of trash and that she thought we might win. After a while, I noticed some of the stuff we found: cigarettes, candy and gum wrappers, paper, pens, and other neat but dirty stuff like that.

When our fifteen minutes were up we brought our trash to the gym. Our teacher said we shouldn't add the cardboard because we had collected enough trash, but we insisted. Finally we got her to agree. Afterward we went to the restroom, washed our hands, and went back to class.

The results of the contest would be told to the school at the end of the day, over the loudspeaker. While we were in class, some parents who had volunteered to help weighed the trash to determine who had the most. When the winner was announced over the loudspeaker, to my bewilderment, my class had won.

I do not go to that school anymore, but my family lives right next to it. Sometimes my sister, our friend Jessica, and I go back to the school grounds to see if there is any trash to pick up. Sometimes when people see us picking up trash, they join us. Once we saw so much trash we had to go back and get more bags. We are never really able to pick up all the trash, but what we do pick up helps a lot.

Our school is only one little area on this earth, but if every school, club, Girl and Boy Scout troop, family, and company did what we did, think how much cleaner the world would be.

Planting Trees

....

Paris Collier, age 12

LIFE IS VALUABLE. THAT IS WHY I HELP PLANT TREES.

Last year and the year before, at school, each student got some baby trees to take home. My great aunt took them and planted them by her house. Since then, a big storm came and ripped them all out of the ground, so my grandma and I planted some adolescent trees in her yard this summer.

Many people neglect trees even though they are very valuable to us. They give us oxygen, shade, beautiful scenery, and homes for the animals. Every one of these helps people in some way. I think everyone should thank the trees by planting more of them. We have already chopped down millions of trees. I say, why wait for trees to be chopped down to plant more?

I think everyone should be like a bird and start planting seeds of trees or even trees themselves. Remember, all those beautiful pictures of landscapes were inspired by real-life landscapes, probably more beautiful than the pictures they inspired.

Recycling for a Better World

....

Christi Lynn, age 11

I HAVE MADE THE WORLD BETTER BY RECYCLING.

My family and I recycle glass bottles, milk cartons, cardboard, newspapers, and cans. We also recycle all biodegradable materials by composting them. We recycle leaves and grass clippings by composting them. Recycling is very important because it saves space in landfills and reuses the earth's resources. They won't last forever!

I have also made the world better by giving some of my toys and clothes to the homeless. I share my things with less fortunate people because I have so much. It must be very nice for them to get things when they really need them.

This is what I have done to make the world a better place.

Saving the Rain Forests

....

Matt Collins, age 13

OUR FOURTH-GRADE CLASS WORKED TO SAVE A RAIN FOREST IN South America. To make the world a better place, we raised enough money to save a portion of it.

We earned money by dusting the furniture at Arhaus Furniture. We shuffled around the store cleaning every piece of furniture in sight. The owner of the furniture store donated money to save the rain forest for all our hard work that day. The owner also treated us to lunch—pizza and pop. Each of us received a long-sleeved T-shirt that said SAVE THE RAIN FOREST!

Our class was also on the news that night. A few of us were interviewed about our class project. We told the reporter about the importance of protecting our environment.

I learned about the importance of the rain forest by participating in this project. Before we dusted furniture, we studied rain forests. We learned what a rain forest is, where they are in the world, and why it's important to protect them. I was curious about rain forests, so I did some research.

"Rain forest" refers to a primary forest in regions with more than one-hundred inches of rainfall per year! They are important for their trees. In the tropics, rain forest trees provide crops like rubber, tea, coffee, bananas, and sugar cane.

There are two major types of rain forests: temperate and tropical. A tropical rain forest has broadleaf evergreen trees, lots of vines, and a lot of plant and animal life. Tropical rain forests are in abundance in the Amazon Basin of South America, Africa, Southeast Asia, Central America, and Australia. Temperate rain forests grow in higher latitudes with wet climates. They are found on the northwest coast of North America, in southern Chile, and in New Zealand. Rain forests cover less than six percent of the earth's total land surface.

People have destroyed many rain forests in our world. They have cut down the trees for timber or to plant crops. The problem is, trees grow very slowly, so we need to protect the ones we have today. All living things need plants to survive. We need to protect our environment to make our world a better place.

We had fun cleaning furniture that day, but we also did something worthwhile. I wish we had prolonged our study of the rain forests. It was my favorite fourth-grade unit. Now that I know about rain forests, I pay more attention to rain forest stories on the news or in the newspaper.

Saratoga

....

Nicolette L. Svestka, age 12

IT ALL STARTED WHEN MY PARENTS GOT US THE MOVIE *FREE Willy*, a story about a whale that was in captivity and a little boy who helped set him free.

At the beginning of the movie, people talked about how the whale population was falling because they were being killed for their skin. They also told us all the good reasons to adopt a whale. So, my brothers and I told our parents that we wanted to adopt one. They said they would give it some thought.

After a week, my parents said we could adopt a whale. We watched the beginning of the movie again to find out how. My dad called the number advertised in the movie and got the information. When my dad got off the phone, he said we needed to send in $30 and our names. That was all they needed! It would take four to seven weeks to get information about our whale.

Six weeks later, we received the name of our whale, where they were going to keep her, how old she was, and how much she weighed. Saratoga was about three years old, and she weighed about five short tons. She was found near Orlando, Florida. We got a picture of her and a report on how she was doing. Saratoga now lives in Florida at a marina for hurt or adopted animals.

I was so glad that we got to adopt a whale. They are endangered and I would like them to be around when my children have children. I hope that more and more people will wake up and see what is happening to our environment and realize that we need to do something about it.

I know that the rain forests, forests everywhere, and the jungles are being destroyed for paper and other things made from trees. Farmland and living space is also needed, but we just can't go and destroy anything or any place just to have it. The plants and animals need a place to live and food to eat, just like us.

That's why I adopted a whale, so people of the future can have something to look at—maybe to have as a pet, if their parents don't mind—and so they have something they can learn about in school, just like I did.

Please, try to do something about the endangered plants and animals. I know I'm going to try. Are you?

Zip-A-Dee-Doo-Dah

*Julia C. Villa, age 17; Maria LaPlante, age 17;
Jessica Roeder, age 17; Jamie Lisagor, age 18;
and Elizabeth Rha, age 17*

THE ONE THING THAT STICKS IN MY MIND WAS HOW COLD IT was that day. I was wearing jeans, a T-shirt, a long-sleeved shirt, a sweatshirt, and warm-ups, and I was still freezing. But nothing was going to stop the five of us from cleaning up the trash in Great Falls Park.

Things didn't start off so well. We couldn't seem to find any trash. To keep our spirits up we began singing. Our numbers ranged from "Zip-A-Dee-Doo-Dah" to "Brown-Eyed Girl" to "Wannabe" by the Spice Girls. As we climbed all over the slippery rocks in search of trash, our melodious voices echoed throughout the park. Then we struck gold.

As we stood upon some rocks looking around for trash, a little distance away we saw bottles, cups, wrappers—the works. As we hurried to our gold mine of trash, our songs died out. We were far too excited about our find. You would have thought we had struck real gold. When we finally arrived at the trash deposit, our frozen fingers began placing items in our garbage bags. The trash didn't seem to stop. We just kept putting more and more trash in our bags. It was saddening that people would leave so much trash on the rocks. Things got brighter when we finished digging for trash. We began a round of "John Jacob Jingle Highmer Schmidt."

Then the most marvelous thing happened. People around us began helping out when they realized what we were doing. Some hikers pointed out more trash to us. Another family actually joined in and helped us pick up the trash. It was remarkable how we could get the rest of the community to rally together. I guess everyone realizes the ugliness of litter.

After a few hours, it was time to go back. As we walked back to the nature center, people thanked us for our efforts. Singing more songs by the Spice Girls on the way to the car, we knew it had been truly worth it, even if we were freezing.

How I Help the World

....

Jean Beagle, age 7

WHEN I WAS A BABY, MY MOM AND DAD WOULD PUSH ME IN A baby jogger. We would pick up soda cans while my mom and dad ran. Before I could talk, whenever I saw a can I would point to it. It was fun picking up cans. We ran a lot of miles and picked up many cans.

When I was five, I went camping with my mom, dad, and a friend at Bastrop State Park. The first night, we went for a bike ride. I rode on my dad's bike. There was so much trash that the road did not look pretty. The second day, when we went for a run along the same road, we picked up all the cans—about one hundred of them. The road looked much prettier when we went home.

I am now too big for the baby jogger. But I still pick up cans wherever we go, and my mom and dad still bring back cans from their runs.

We store the cans behind and inside our garage. When I was very little, we would take the cans after church to a can cruncher in a store parking lot. It was fun hearing all the cans crunching, but it was messy. Now we store the cans until we get a lot of them, then we take them on our friend's big truck to the recycling place.

One time, I sold 410 pounds at once. I have sold over 1,000 pounds of cans, and I am only seven years old.

I help the world by making the roads, the lakes, and the trails prettier, and because all my cans are recycled.

Baby Birds

....

Tara Digregorio, age 13

I HELPED MAKE THE WORLD A BETTER PLACE BY HELPING SOME baby birds in our yard.

I didn't know how to feed them and take care of them, so we called the vet to see how. The vet said to feed them cat food soaked in water. I did that. Every night when they would chirp, I had to get up at 1:00 A.M., 2:00 A.M., and so on, to feed them. Finally, we took them to the vet where they would learn how to fly.

We found baby birds every summer. I would be walking outside and I would hear chirping. When I would look down, there would be more baby birds. I think we found them every year because they lived in our dryer vent where the heat went out. The mom probably dropped them out because it got too hot, especially in the summer!

One time I was taking care of the baby birds and one stopped eating. I would try to put food in its mouth, but it wouldn't swallow. Then its breathing changed. I could tell it was catching a cold. I started covering it with a little cover and would check it every night, but it didn't help. After a couple of days, it died.

I was sad about the baby bird that died, but at least I helped many others. It was a really good experience.

HELPING THOSE IN NEED

The Homeless Shelter

T. J. Dubil, age 12

ONE SUMMER, CURTIS PENN, MY FRIENDS EDDIE AND JOEY, and I were in the park playing football when we saw a homeless guy sitting on a nearby park bench. He started walking toward us. He was sort of a scrubby looking man about 5 foot 6 and around 150 pounds. He asked us if we knew much about football. We talked to him for a little bit and he told us his name was Mr. Paterno. "But you can call me Joe," he said.

Our friendship with Joe grew within the next week or so, to the point where we visited him daily. We would talk to him and run plays that he used in college when he played quarterback. At the end of the summer, Joey moved to Nebraska. When Joey moved, Eddie and I started a shelter for the homeless people in the old school building.

It became a success. Within the next year, Mr. Paterno had a bunch of job interviews with the board office, but he decided to coach football. The next season, when Eddie and I signed up for football, Mr. Paterno was our coach. We went 6 and 1 and were second in the league. The only team we did not beat was Kilbourne Middle School. It was a great year.

As the years went by, Joe got tired of coaching middle school and applied to Penn State. A week later, he got a letter saying he was accepted.

I feel I had something to do with Joe's life changing. If my friends and I hadn't talked to him in the park that day, it never would have happened.

Grandma's Gifts

Sean Saffell, age 13

EMILY DOUGLAS IS DOING A GREAT THING FOR OUR WORLD. Helped by Sara and Zach, her younger brother and sister, Emily, who is fifteen years old, has organized a program called Grandma's Gifts. This program sets up educational programs and sends food, clothing, and books to needy children in Ohio, Kentucky, and West Virginia.

Emily started Grandma's Gifts a few years ago. Emily started this program because her grandmother was very poor when she was young. Her grandmother's father died at a very young age, leaving twelve children in all. Her grandmother was teased because she would wear the same pink dress to church every Sunday. When she grew up, Emily's grandmother donated things to the poor children in her small town of Ironton. After Emily's grandmother died, Emily decided to continue that legacy and give to needy children in the community.

Grandma's Gifts started as a very small operation but it has grown to be very large. At first, Emily bought everything herself. After a lot of publicity, Emily is now getting many donations. What started as a community effort in the town of Ironton, which is in the southeastern part of Ohio, has spread to parts of eastern Kentucky and northwestern West Virginia.

Last year, Emily received a national teenage volunteer award from President Clinton for Grandma's Gifts. Only a handful of other kids were presented this prestigious award. She was invited to a national meeting for volunteers by the president himself and got to eat dinner with the president and other former presidents. Her picture appeared in *Time Magazine*.

I think Emily has done a great thing for our country by helping children get basic necessities. She is providing things that most kids in our world take for granted, like schoolbooks, shoes, toiletries, and nice clothing. It's awesome.

There is no way you can put into words how much she has helped these children. Emily is doing a great thing for these kids, and I hope she continues for the rest of her life.

A Merrier Christmas

....

Sarah Adams, age 12

I WAS IN A GIRL SCOUT TROOP FROM KINDERGARTEN TO THE beginning of sixth grade. It was made up of mostly the same girls each year. We always found different ways to help others.

My favorite project was one we did every year around Christmas. My group would sponsor one or two needy families through the Clintonville Community Resource Center. We would get a list of the needy families with the name and age of each child in the family, along with three to five things that child wanted for Christmas. We also got information about the parent or parents. Each girl in my group bought a couple of presents for the children. Each child could only get three presents, so that no child got more than another. We were supposed to spend only $30 on each child. We made sure the parents got gifts, too. The moms received mostly jewelry, soaps, and perfumes, while the dads got socks, cologne, books, and gloves.

My group also bought food for the family's Christmas dinner. We gave them a gift certificate to buy turkey, mashed potatoes, and the makings for pie. We also gave them canned foods such as green beans, carrots, potatoes, beans, sweet potatoes, and Jell-O and pudding mixes.

When the girls in my group had finished purchasing the presents, we all gathered at one of our houses to wrap each gift and have a Christmas party. We labeled who the gift was for but left a space for the parents to sign, as though it was from them. That way, the children would not know that their parents needed help to get them presents. A few days later, my group would take the presents to a collection site, usually a school. Each year, the school's gym was almost filled with gifts for many different families. We usually brought the gifts in laundry baskets so that the families could carry all their gifts home.

Every Christmas when I open my presents, I don't think about the families we have helped because I am usually too excited about the gifts I am getting. But afterward, I feel bad that I got so many presents while they only got three. I do feel good, though, that I am one of the people who helped them get their presents and Christmas dinner.

Sometimes I wonder if the families still use the things that we got them. I wonder what happened to them. Did they get a new job, or marry someone with more money, or are they still poor? I hope they liked their presents and had a fun day, because I had fun helping them have a merrier Christmas.

How the Girl Scouts Helped the Homeless

Anonymous, age 12

WE GATHERED AT OUR USUAL PLACE, UNITED METHODIST. Our leader told us to go down to the kitchen, set the tables, and get the food ready. Then she told us what was going on—it was our turn to help the homeless.

My fellow Girl Scouts and I spent a couple of hours preparing the meal. The lady in charge of the project helped, too. We were excited and nervous at the same time. I was nervous because I had never really seen a homeless person before. I didn't know what they looked like, or how they acted.

When the homeless came, they were dressed in clothes like we wear, just not as stylish. There were kids our age, too. I was excited when I saw how cute the children were. I couldn't wait to play with them. We got to eat with them and have dessert. We had chicken, potatoes, beans, cookies, cake—all kinds of good stuff. After we ate, we played with the children. We played Hide and Go Seek, Tag, Follow the Leader, and Freeze Tag.

When we were about to leave, one of the kids didn't want us to go. But we said good-bye and told him we would be back. All of us had fun. As we left, I said a little prayer that people all over would help the homeless and take care of them.

I felt proud of what I did. I think my troop really helped.

Never Will I Stop

....

Kevin Hautala, age 12

IT ALL STARTED WHEN MY MOM FELT IT WAS TIME TO QUIT HER job and make the world a better place. Our whole family of four looked into doing foster care. We wanted to help children in need.

The decision was made. We first did respite care, to give other parents a break. After a while, we got a phone call for our first permanent foster care children, my brother and sister. When they arrived, we were all enthusiastic. They were shy at first, but after a couple of days we saw their wonderful personalities. They stayed with us for awhile and they had a wonderful time.

After about six months, they were supposed to go back to their parent. They didn't, even though it looked like they would many times. Eventually, we signed some papers. All of us, including me, agreed to adopt them. After about a year, they became a permanent part of our loving family. I felt a wonderful joy in my heart.

Another thing I have done to help the earth is picking up trash. When I was in fourth grade, all I could see was the ugly, disgusting park covered with trash. The awful smell and messy look really bothered me. So I grabbed a big garbage bag and started picking up the cigarette butts, candy wrappers, and other dirty things. After a while, other people started to help me. It was a lot of bending my back and hard work. But after a couple of hours, the park looked magnificent.

I love to help save the earth, and I love being myself. Never will I stop helping other people around me. There are a lot of people who want to help save the world, but a lot of people have no respect for the world. Someday the world will need everybody to respect and help it in order for it to be a wonderful place.

A Christmas Gift

Lindsey Meyer, age 12

THIS PAST CHRISTMAS, MY FAMILY AND I "ADOPTED" A FAMILY through a fund entitled Adopt-a-Family. I don't think people realize how many people are poor, homeless, or just can't afford to buy their children Christmas or birthday presents! I don't think my family noticed either, until we enrolled in the Adopt-a-Family foundation.

Adopt-a-Family is a fund for people who can't afford Christmas presents for their family. People who want to help other families can enroll through their church.

The family we adopted was just a mother and her daughter. They lived in an apartment with just the bare minimum. Yes, they had a car. But many people don't. What surprised me was that even though they didn't have much money, the mother still went to church. You would think she would be working twenty-four hours a day, seven days a week. Someone that poor who still goes to church—that is a true Christian. Then again, maybe that is why she does have a car, an apartment, and why she met us!

We enjoyed meeting this nice lady and her daughter. We bought them a bunch of gifts. Shopping for them was enjoyable, so was giving them the gifts. But the best part was how good it made me feel about myself.

Lucky and Unlucky

....

Candace Berge, age 12

ALL MY LIFE I'VE HEARD ABOUT THE DIFFERENCE PEOPLE MAKE in others' lives by showing them they care.

Of course, I've done minor things to help, like donating clothes to the Salvation Army or buying a gift for someone who really needs it, I just never thought that those things actually affected lives.

When I was in third grade, my mom and I would visit the nursing home. I remember my mom telling me how much elderly people enjoy seeing a young person, and that it was good for them to have something to look forward to every Sunday.

At Christmastime for as long as I can remember, my mom has chosen two cards from the Christmas tree at her work. These cards have the names of children whose parents can't afford to buy them many toys—if any—along with something small they would like to get for Christmas. The card my mom picked for me this year was a four-year-old girl who asked only for a small jar of Play-Dough! I couldn't believe it. Of all the things she could have asked for, she asked for such a small thing. Of course, my mom and I decided to get her a lot more than that. I only wish I could have been there to see the look on her face when she unwrapped all her gifts.

Thinking about Christmas, I sometimes end up bringing my own few dollars with me to the grocery store so I can drop them off in the Salvation Army bucket. My admiration goes out to those who volunteer to stand outside in the cold to help raise money for those who need it.

Another thing I have done to help the world involves smoking. It has always bothered me, but it really got to me when I found out that my cousin Emily had been smoking for almost a year. She was my favorite cousin and I couldn't just let it slide by. I reminded her what could happen if she continued to smoke, and she decided to quit. She has been smoke-free for about a year now!

I know that inconsequential things like this don't make a huge difference, but I believe that if everyone would do one nice thing for someone else, it would make the world a much better place. After all, some of us are lucky, but some of us aren't.

The World and Its People

....

Jenna Gazelka, age 12

I THINK EVERYBODY SHOULD DO SOMETHING FOR THE WORLD or the people in the world. There are many ways you can help. My family helps the poor and homeless by giving them clothes that we don't need anymore.

When I give a family my clothes, I feel like I have just given them a million dollars. When you help the poor or homeless, you make their lives less difficult. It's so easy to help someone. You just have to have the willpower and strength to do so. You also need to take the time. It took me one whole day to get all my old clothes folded and packed and ready to go. When you have the time, you should sit down and make someone's life better or make the world a better place.

By helping the poor and homeless, I have helped to make the world better. It made me feel like a better person, and it will make you feel like a better person, too. If you help the world or a person in it, you will feel better about yourself and it will give you self-confidence.

Helping the Homeless

David P. Johnston, age 13

TWICE EVERY YEAR, MY FAMILY AND A COUPLE OTHERS GO OUT to help the poor.

We take food for them. We always take about twenty boxes of Krispy cream doughnuts, and by the next day they are gone.

I love going, because they are nice, funny, and all around good people. I wish I could go every day. The poor people enjoy it and often make jokes. One time, I met this guy. He was asking me all kinds of questions. He said I was pretty cool and told me to come back. Ever since, whenever I go, I've gone back to look for him.

I like going there, it's pretty fun. And it's nice to know I'm helping someone else out.

Helping Those in Need   69

A Gift

....

NMD, age 11

I'VE ALWAYS BEEN KIND OF A CARING PERSON. BUT MY MOM IS the one who helped me to reach out and help others.

When my siblings and I started earning money, my mom said that ten percent of our earnings should go to a college fund and another ten percent to charity. She also said that we could choose the charity. The ones she listed were children who don't get presents at Christmas, war-torn countries, and homeless shelters.

It took me a long time to decide. One night when I was going to speed skating, we had to go through St. Paul. I saw kids sleeping under the overpass. I tried not to look, but I just couldn't help it. I just stared at them, feeling so sorry for them. Then I remembered seeing two people in Northtown, each holding a sign that said "I will work for food." I remembered how sorry I felt for them.

That night I decided where my money would go—the homeless. So when I got home I told my mom what I had decided. We sent ten percent of the money I made from mowing lawns last summer to a homeless shelter.

Maybe I'll get that same job again and do the same thing next year. Or maybe I'll pick a different charity. Either way, I will feel good knowing I've done something on my own to help someone.

COMPANIONSHIP

Elsie

....

Anna Evenson, age 11

ONE EVENING, WHEN THE SUN WAS JUST OVER THE HORIZON, Anna's mother said, "Anna, will you please take this grape jelly to Elsie?"

"You know, Mom, I'm extremely busy." Anna was watching her favorite television show, Home Improvement. It had just started.

"Just do it, please?" Anna's mother begged.

"Fine, just as long as it takes five minutes." Anna grabbed the jelly from the counter, put on her coat, and slammed the door.

As she trudged through the thick, white snow, she wondered what was happening on her TV show, but was interrupted by the loud barks of her dog, Mickey. It was probably because he was hungry.

Finally, Anna reached Elsie's house. It was a cream color with a porch painted the color of a cross between brick and maroon. The paint on the porch was chipping away. Someone needed to repaint it, Anna thought to herself.

As Anna walked up the cement steps, she could hear the TV going full blast. It sounded like one of those old shows on public television, with a band that plays old-fashioned music. She knocked. Elsie peeked through the window to see who had rapped at the door. You could see the wrinkles on her face. Elsie was old. She was a short lady with silvery gray hair. She had long arms, and glasses that looked way too big for her face. She disappeared from behind the window and opened the door. "Hello! How are you?" Elsie asked.

"Just great," Anna replied.

"Come on in!" Elsie exclaimed. Anna walked through the door and put the jam on the table.

"I brought you some grape jelly," she said.

"Why, thank you," Elsie replied.

Anna looked at the television. She had been right—it was one of those old-time shows. Anna sat down at the kitchen table, and Elsie turned off the TV. They talked for about fifteen minutes. Elsie asked how school was going, whether Anna had gone ice skating yet this year, and how the family was doing. Anna politely answered "just fine," "yes," or "sure" to Elsie's questions. As she looked at the clock, Anna saw that it was 6:45 P.M.—still enough time to watch the end of her show. She got up, and she and Elsie said their good-byes.

As Anna walked out the door, she heard Elsie say, "Come back again!" Anna looked back, and Elsie waved good-bye. She was smiling. Anna smiled back and started on her way home.

Anna couldn't help but notice the tingle of joy she felt seeing Elsie's smile, the kind of joy you feel when you've done a good deed. Anna had actually made someone else happy!

When Anna got home, supper was ready. It was her favorite dish, chicken and rice. Yum! Anna tore off her jacket and sat at the egg-shaped table. She chowed down her meal and then went to her room.

Freshly-painted walls and new Pooh wallpaper were there to greet her. It was 8:30 P.M.—time to get ready for bed. For Anna, getting up in the morning was a chore.

• • •

BEEP! BEEP! BEEP! It was 6:07 A.M. The alarm seemed especially loud this morning. Anna moaned as she got out of bed. She went into the bathroom to wash her face. This always woke her up in the morning. Anna returned to her room to get dressed. Today she chose a pair of jeans, a striped T-shirt, and the Eeyore sweatshirt she had received for Christmas. By now, she was feeling more awake.

Anna smelled freshly brewed coffee as she walked into the kitchen for breakfast. Anna took a kiwi out of the plastic bag on top of the microwave, peeled it with a razor-sharp knife, and gulped it down. She looked at the clock. It was 7:20 A.M. She had time to go over to Elsie's house.

"Mom, I'm going to go over to Elsie's to play my violin." Her mother whirled around in surprise. She didn't think Anna was serious, but when her mother saw she wasn't kidding, she let Anna go.

Anna went to her room to grab her violin and her favorite piece of music, *La Folia*. The music had variety. It was fast, with lots of feeling in the slow movements. The music was like Anna, in a way. She knew she was a little different, with all sorts of different feelings inside her. "'Bye, Mom!" she said as she walked out the door.

Anna walked through the white snow up to Elsie's house. She knocked. Finally, Elsie came to the door and let Anna in. Anna played her piece. It sounded incredible. It was even better than when she had practiced it at home. When she finished, Anna explained that an author was coming to their school, so she'd better not be late. She packed her violin, grabbed her school bag, and walked out to the car. Her mother was taking her to school.

School went by fast that day. The author, Ben Mikaelson, was awesome. At least, that was what Anna thought. He talked about his life and how he came to be an author. It was fun to listen to someone so interesting.

. . .

Back home, Anna ran into the house and practically tore off the refrigerator door. She looked on the second shelf—there was some raspberry jam left. Grabbing it, she headed over to Elsie's house. It was a short visit. She dropped off the jam and started for home. When Elsie asked why she couldn't stay longer, Anna replied, "I have to start supper."

"Come again!" Elsie called after her. Anna smiled. It was nice to have someone who wanted her to visit so often.

. . .

At 6:45 P.M., supper was ready. Anna and her brother, Elliot, sat down with their parents to enjoy the chicken soup Anna had made. It was so hot it burned her tongue. Waiting for it to cool, Anna said, "It's kind of nice to have an old lady by your house. You can make her happy. It's nice to know someone enjoys talking to you."

"It doesn't hurt to take some of your time to please other people," Anna's mom said. "It not only makes them happy, it makes you feel good inside, too."

"I guess you're right," Anna said. "It doesn't hurt at all!"

From that day on, Anna took the time to visit Elsie. They talked, laughed, played games, and listened to music together. Anna learned that it feels good to make someone else happy. Anna and Elsie became good friends and are still close to this day. They will probably be friends forever!

A Different View

Elyse Zavar, age 13

THROUGH A GROUP ORGANIZATION, A COUPLE OF FRIENDS AND I went to the School for the Blind for a day. In preparation for our visit, we were told to respond to the blind children as we would respond to children without a disability. When we arrived at the school, each of us was matched with a buddy. We stayed with our buddies for the entire day to help us see what a day at their school was like.

Not all of the kids at the school were totally blind. Some had a slight loss of sight, while others were completely blind. Some of the kids had other problems too. My buddy, Daniel, was partially blind, but he also had a problem with his joints.

Daniel was five years old, and his class schedule was full of fun activities. We first went to Daniel's art class where we got to do finger painting. The next activity was in the gym, a soft room with mats all over, and a huge ball you could jump on and roll over. Daniel said that this class was his favorite. The room also had a mini-slide, a soft jungle gym, and an obstacle course. The activity planned for us was a game where everyone was blind. A ball was passed to all of the players and the only way you could catch the ball was by using your ears to find it. We then went to a special dance movement class to help Daniel strengthen his joints and muscles. The kids in this class moved around a lot and they had a lot of fun!

Finally, it was time for lunch. Like at most schools, the food was not too good. When we finished eating, we went outside.

There my friends and I discussed our day at the school so far. Everyone said they were having fun and enjoying the program. We all wanted to come back and do it again.

Next, Daniel and I went to his music class to play instruments. The younger kids performed a song they had prepared for us. My friends and I were very impressed with their little musical. After the kids finished their performance we went again to the play gym where we goofed around for about forty-five minutes. We all had a good time.

Too soon it was time to say good-bye. Spending a day at the School for the Blind was like a snapshot of what it is like to be blind. I had only met Daniel that morning, but we had already formed a friendship. After my friends and I left the school, I felt lucky that I had my sight, but I also felt lucky that I had gotten to meet Daniel and all the other kids. It helped me realize that even though Daniel was different in some ways, we were also very similar in lots of other ways. He wanted to be with friends and have fun, just like everyone else.

I know that I will never forget Daniel, or my experiences at the school. Sometimes when you take a chance and spend the time to learn about someone who is different from yourself, you can see how differences don't really matter. In some cases, those differences can make that person special.

The World and I

....

Laura Nygaard, age 12

EVEN THOUGH I HAVEN'T DONE SOMETHING MAJOR TO MAKE the world a better place, I have done some things. They aren't much, but they came from my heart.

I really like to be outdoors. Lately, at my cabin, I've been seeing a lot of gun shells. So one day I decided to pick up all the trash I found while taking a walk. Boy, was there a ton of trash! I found about a dozen gun shells, a bunch of paper, and even a tire that I pulled out of the lake! It made me feel better that day. I could have saved an animal or two from choking on one of the pieces of trash.

One of my teachers does volunteer work for elderly people whose relatives don't visit them anymore. Every major holiday, my class and I decorate bags for these people. Then my teacher and her volunteer group put little candies and food in the bags we decorated. It makes the elderly happy to see our drawings, so I feel better that I made someone happier.

My grandparents and great-grandparents tend to feel lonely sometimes. I visit them so they have something to look forward to. It makes me feel special when I visit them. They feel special, too, so I think I am helping them live a better life. Knowing that, I can rest better.

When I'm older, I'm going to be a doctor, a vet, or someone that helps others. So I work hard to get good grades in school, and I do all my homework. If I could be a doctor and find a cure for cancer, that would help the world a lot.

This world needs a lot of things. We need people who under-stand nature and know how important it is, and we need doctors to find a cure for cancer. Someday I hope to do something major to help the world. I'm doing lots of little things now, but I hope I can do more.

Project Uplift

Ashley Chaddock, age 13; Patricia Cunningham, age 13; Corey Ingram, age 13; and Rynnie Ross, age 13

HI. WE ARE FOUR THIRTEEN-YEAR-OLD GIRLS WHO CAME TO-gether to make a difference in the lives of others. At first, we wanted to do an FHA project. Our teacher, Mrs. Underwood, gave us a planning guide and told us to brainstorm ideas. Then she told us to choose one and see if it fit with any of the FHA purposes. Our project provided opportunities for personal growth and development, promoted greater understanding between youth and adults, provided opportunities for making decisions and assuming responsibilities, and promoted FHA in our community. We began on March 25, 1997. We decided to call our project "Project Uplift."

To start, we set up an appointment with LeAnn Perry, the activities director of what was then Presbyterian Manor. We were all scared and nervous that we wouldn't be able to volunteer. LeAnn told us that they usually didn't accept volunteers of such a young age, but she decided to make an exception for us. We would be able to "adopt" six of the residents. Our adopted grandparents would be Ruth Eisenhuth, Alma Ferguson, Vernon Martin, Ezra Miller, Columbus "Curly" Mills, and Alice Montabone.

Ruth is a sweet lady who is very active and very nice. She loves to play bingo and dominoes, go to parties, do sing-a-longs, exercise, give and get manicures, and participate in many other activities. She loves to talk about her family, her old house, and her life. During this past year, Ruth was hospitalized on her birthday due to pneumonia, but she quickly recovered.

Alma Ferguson is a friendly lady who likes dominoes, bingo, and manicures. The first party we threw was for Alma. We got her flowers, a big stuffed bunny, a cake, and a balloon we lost on the way. Alma was very surprised, and the party was a great success. Alma has relatives who visit often. They are always thanking us for spending time with her.

Vernon Martin is an interesting man from New Zealand. He has lots of stories, and we can always strike up a conversation with him. He spends most of the day in the third-floor day room. Vernon's birthday is October 31. We missed his birthday, so we are going to try to make it up to him. We visit him a lot because he doesn't seem to like crowds and activities.

Ezra Clay Miller is very active and loves to watch, play, and talk about sports. He likes to participate in activities such as bingo, birthday parties, and outings. He loves to talk about his family. His sister lives right next door. She loves to come and visit. Ezra is always in a good mood; we enjoy being around him. He tells us about how his granddaughter is one of the best piano players in the country, or how he was in a concentration camp during World War II, or when he cut President Eisenhower's hair. He is very interesting.

Curly Mills is another of our grandparents we always enjoy. He has a great sense of humor and always makes us laugh. Curly suffered some strokes, but that never seems to get him down. He was born on July 31, and we threw him a surprise party that he really enjoyed. We got him an ice cream cake and presents, which included cologne and other little things. We decorated the third-floor day room with streamers, balloons, and even a banner. He always has a smile on his face when we see him.

Alice Montabone was one of our grandparents, but she was doing so well that she was able to go home. We were happy for her, but we all miss her very much.

In addition to visiting our adopted grandparents, we help out with activities for all the residents. We help the activities director call out the numbers at bingo, and we write out coupons for the bingo store or pass out points to those who are playing. We always have a really good time. We also go around to talk to the bedridden patients, give them in-room manicures, read stories, and play games that will help them with hand-eye coordination. These residents hardly ever get a chance to get out to the activities, so we bring the activities to them.

On the second Tuesday of every month, a birthday party is held, and all of the residents are encouraged to attend. When we first began volunteering, a man and a woman came in to sing and play the piano, but in December they quit, leaving the nursing home in a sticky situation. We decided we would take on the challenge and perform at the birthday party. It was a huge success. All of the residents loved it. We had a terrific time also.

These are just a few of the activities we help with. Each month brings something different and special. In all, we have volunteered 165 hours. Our project has been a lot of fun, but we've learned a lot, too. We have learned to get along with people of all ages, a skill that will definitely help us in the future. We have learned what it means to have a true friendship. We have matured both mentally and emotionally. We have learned to work as a group and a team. Most of all, we have learned that everyone needs a friend and someone to talk to.

The reason we chose to call our project "Project Uplift" is because we thought it symbolized our reason for doing this project—to make everyone's day a little bit brighter. We have always been welcomed with open arms, and have cherished every moment spent there. We are all proud to be a part of Project Uplift. The people there are like family to us now.

Touching the Lives of Others

Shannon Winholtz, age 11

ON DECEMBER 16, 1997, MY COUSIN LUKE WAS BORN. December 18, 1997, Luke had a SIDS attack and died two days later. The whole family struggled to accept it. Everybody comforted each other. I wrote letters to Luke's parents, and I still do. I think it helps them a lot.

I also help the elderly. I know that people in nursing homes feel pretty lonely. My teacher had us decorate bags and put treats in them for the elderly people. I really enjoy coloring the bags. I think it works out nicely.

Almost every Sunday, I go to the 9:45 A.M. service at church. Then I work in the nursery during the 11:00 A.M. service. There are a lot of crying and screaming kids, but I like kids a lot. When I take care of some kids, they stop their tantrums. Others scream the whole time because they just want their parents. The majority of the kids don't cry or anything, which is nice. When I work in the nursery, I know I'm helping out a lot of people.

Since I like kids so much, I go to my grandpa's farm to baby-sit my other cousin, Freddie, ten months, who lives nearby. I love going there. We play Peekaboo and ride his little fire truck. When Freddie isn't there for me to baby-sit, I take care of my grandpa. A few months ago, Grandpa had surgery on his eye. My mom drove him around and I went with her. While my mom was parking or just not around, I stayed with him. We get along well together and it's good for us to spend time together. I know I'm helping out when I'm with him.

Around Christmastime, there was a terrible accident in my town. Two girls got hit by a car. It was tragic. Even though I didn't know them, I wrote a sympathy card to the family. I felt it was important for the family to know I cared.

Just for a fun thing in school, we wrote letters to soldiers. Mine went to a soldier in Bosnia. I got a response back a couple of months later. No one had to keep writing, but I did. That soldier and I have been writing back and forth for a long time. It is fun, and I think it helps him for us to be pen pals.

I know these things help make the world a better place, even if they are small.

Finding Friends

Kelly Finkowski, age 11

I JOINED A 4-H CLUB TWO YEARS AGO. SINCE I THOUGHT IT WAS fun, I stayed in it this year. The club has always chosen a community service project or a fun activity to do together each month. This month was a community service project. We were going to a nursing home called Camelia Rose.

We had done this before and I always thought it was fun. We were going to give presentations and would have to talk with the old people after our presentations. When we got there, not everyone in the club was there, so my mom said I should play the piano for them. I didn't have any sheet music and I barely knew the people, but I played anyway. Everyone finally got there and gave their presentations. Then came the time to give out drinks and cookies, and to find someone to talk to.

I stood looking around at all the tables and eventually chose where to start. I asked the people seated at the table how their day was going, but soon found that this wasn't a talkative group. So I turned to the next table and asked the same question. Everyone looked at me as if they couldn't hear or understand what I was saying. Then the lady next to me spoke up.

"Pretty good," she said, smiling. When I looked at her, I decided to stay at this table for a while. She turned out to be a delightful person who was kind and friendly. I started to think of her as a friend, instead of a stranger. I knew it was the same for her, too, because the last time I walked by her, she put a dollar in my hand and said to buy myself a pop. I tried to give it back, but she said to keep it, and that she enjoyed the time with me. Then it was time to go.

This woman, in just a short time, had turned into a friend. As I walked away from the nursing home that afternoon, I realized that if everyone trusted each other like that, we would be well off. I felt I did something good by entertaining people and sharing kindness.

It's Good to Be Me

....

Ryan G. Lanclos, age 17

It is very special to be me. I like who I am. It is the things I do that make up me.

I am an average student who is active in the community. I have been holding a steady job for two years now while still getting all my schoolwork done. I have a really good family that I can look to in times of need. I am very fortunate for all this. I think that some people would prefer to be in my shoes instead of their own.

To help make the world a better place, I have done community service. Every student has to complete at least forty hours of community service to make confirmation. I did most of this by helping my grandmothers around their houses. If every grandchild would help his or her grandparents like I do, it would help make the world a better place.

Also, when I was in the eighth grade, our church group sang carols at a nursing home in our community. The people in the home loved it. It brought smiles to all their faces. It made me feel good inside, too. If people would do this kind of thing more often, the world would be a better place. People in these homes are lonely. Most of them don't have any family left. If people would visit them once in a while, the people in the home would really appreciate it.

These are a few of the things I have done to make the world a better place. These things are really nothing out of the ordinary. Anyone could do them. I am not a bad person, so it isn't too hard for me to make this world better. If there were more people like me, the world would be a lot better than it is today.

GIVING IS BETTER THAN RECEIVING

Caring for the World

Katie Rude, age 12

THERE ARE A NUMBER OF THINGS I HAVE DONE TO MAKE THE world a better place. For one, my family and I helped our church bring a bag full of toys and stuffed animals to a church in St. Paul. That church didn't have enough money to buy the younger kids presents for Christmas. I also gave money to my church to help the missionaries.

I have served food at a homeless shelter and also brought food to my school to give to a shelter. To help my school get new computers and new equipment for the gym, I sold candy and wallpaper around my neighborhood. My family and I also give clothes that don't fit us anymore to the Salvation Army. We have done this more than eleven times.

Sometimes I help out at my mom's work—an assisted living facility—by helping the older patients get to their room from downstairs in the activity room.

I think everybody should care for the world and for other people, mostly because God gave it to us. I am glad I could do something to make the world a better place. Maybe you could use my ideas to help, too.

The Challenge

....

Lanie Michele Broussard, age 18

FOR DAYS AND DAYS, I HAVE THOUGHT ABOUT WHAT MY BIGGEST challenge in life has been, and nothing seemed good enough. Then, as if it were sent from God, it came to me. My biggest challenge was, and still is, high school.

To most people, high school seems like a four-year party, but to me it is very different. You see, I have always had a plan or a sort of vision about ways I could give back to society through my experiences in high school. My mind was filled with "to do" lists, enumerating various projects I would someday like to be part of and people I would someday like to help.

During high school, my challenge every year was not only to succeed academically, but to become involved in as many positive organizations as possible. I wanted to encourage others to give back to our community. This may not seem like a difficult task, but getting a group of teenagers to do anything except party is a challenge in itself.

My plan went into action the fall of 1994. It was my freshman year and I was determined to get involved and make a difference. I began asking older peers to help me become part of the Key Club, which is a service organization into which one must be invited. Finally, the day came when the invitations were sent out. I had been invited! I attended the meetings and organized food drives, clothing collections, and many other projects that aided those in need. During that year, I also ran for the captain of the cheerleading squad and was elected. This may not seem like a position that could help me in my cause, but I saw it as an opportunity to get others involved in my project.

My grandmother always told me, "People must trust and respect you before they will follow you." With this phrase in mind, I diligently worked all year long to get the girls on the squad to respect me and, most of all, trust me. I still had a clear vision of how I would use my high school years to make the world a brighter place by influencing others to spread love and kindness where it was dark and dingy.

When my sophomore year arrived, I was still pursuing my desire to do good. During this year, a student is eligible to be invited into another service organization if he or she meets certain qualifications. The previous year, I strove to keep up my grades and to maintain a respectable reputation; consequently, I was officially invited and inducted into the National Beta Club during my sophomore year. We had meetings once a month and made plans to help out our community in some way. We decided that we would visit the nursing home in our area for Christmas.

The week before the Christmas holidays, we wrapped boxes of tissue and made candy canes and wreath decorations for the elderly. When we arrived, the residents were ecstatic to see us. We decorated their rooms and talked with them for hours about their younger years and their families. That day I walked out of the building with a certain joy and an unexplainable sense of peace. Giving instead of receiving was an amazing concept that had never touched me so deeply before that day.

During my sophomore year, I was again captain of the cheerleading squad. I continued to try to prove to these girls that they could depend on me and follow me. I also learned to be not just a leader, but a friend. I hoped that this would help me to encourage others to reach out to those in desperate need.

My junior year came around rather quickly. My vision had now broadened and I began to involve myself in as many organizations as possible. My reason for this was to get to know as many types of people as I could. I wanted to gather as many experiences as possible and get diverse opinions from people from all walks of life. I got involved in the swim team and soccer team, and I was still a member of the Key Club, Beta Club, and varsity cheerleading squad. These organizations gave me a chance to interact with a variety of students. I was able to get a feel for different personalities and select those whom I thought would aid in my plans.

Another program that I was involved in, along with thirty-nine other students from five area high schools, was Lafayette Junior Leadership. It made a dramatic impact on my life and helped me realize how many organizations, right in our own community, were in need of volunteers, donations, and other types of assistance. I also realized that no matter how insignificant my efforts seemed, I could have changed a person's life forever and not even realized it.

This was a turning point in my life. It was like the snowball effect. The feeling and drive to reach people got greater and greater. I saw the community as a great big hand reaching out for help and guidance.

This year, my senior year, I put my plans and aspirations into full swing. I was elected captain of the cheerleading squad again this year. Through this experience, I have learned how to work with others and persuade them to spread kindness and love to those in need. For Christmas, our entire squad, along with friends and family, bought gifts for the residents of a local children's shelter. The fifteen girls on the squad and I delivered the presents on a bright, sunny afternoon about a week before Christmas. When we walked in, my heart began to glow as I looked at the delighted faces of these lonely, abandoned children. That afternoon we played games with them, sang

Christmas carols, and even performed a cheer or two. The way I felt when they looked at us with a sudden hope and amazement is a feeling that could never be explained with words. It was truly amazing. We hugged each of them before we left and wished them all a Merry Christmas. The girls left the shelter with an enhanced appreciation for life and a serene feeling in their souls, I believe.

For my part, I felt complete and whole again. In giving my time, I received something so much greater. I have continued my journey in helping others, particularly children, by volunteering at my church and at the Faith House, which is a shelter for battered women and children. My high school days are about to end, but my dream of motivating others to spread to others the love and happiness they have received will never die.

Great People

Lani E. Owings, age 13

MY SUNDAY SCHOOL CLASS AND I WENT TO RAKE AT AN ELDER'S house because the person couldn't rake anymore. I'm going to tell you about it, and a little more about helping the world become a better place.

It was fun raking leaves. We raked most of the class time. Some people even gave up their rakes and used their hands or held bags. I raked and held bags. Every once in a while, I would glance away from my work to see what other people were doing. Some worked quietly, some socialized while working, and some just socialized. I socialized while working.

We raked for a long time. It was hard work, but still fun. The leaves would crackle as we raked. There were a lot of leaves to rake, for almost every tree bough was bare. Some of the leaves were blotchy and had spots of different colors. The leaves were all different colors and sizes. Some larger, some smaller. Most of the people worked very hard. The teachers thought that was great. We had a good time.

There are many good people in our world and most of them have helped someone else or helped the environment. Some ways to help someone else: cut their grass, rake their leaves, shovel their snow. Some ways to help the environment: recycle, pick up trash, save the animals, don't pollute. I bet you are one of those good people who has done one of these things.

Most good people would do these things without accepting payment. Most people just do nice things for other people and the environment out of the goodness of their heart. I find these people very touching. Even if you do something nice as part of a group—like with your class—you would be considered great. Even though we never met her, the person we raked for thought it was very considerate of us to help her out.

If you do something good, you'll feel good about it. I know I have. Do something nice and make God happy. You are all great people and God would like to see you do nice things. Help your elders, your friends, your relatives, and all your peers. Suggest to your teacher that you want your class to help someone or to do something for the environment. Form a caring club.

If you help someone or the environment, it will show to your friends. What you do can show people how good you really are. It's not being a showoff, either. It's a great thing to do.

I look up to people who help other people and the environment. Other young people look up to elders who help as well. If everyone helps out, soon the world will be a more peaceful place. The world is a peaceful place now, but we want it to be even better. If you want the world to be a better place, help other people and help the environment. It's a nice thing to do. Be considered a great person. Show people how good you really are.

The Spirit of Christmas

Lauren Cattell, age 13

I HAVE ALWAYS BEEN FORTUNATE ENOUGH TO HAVE A NICE cooked dinner waiting for me and a big Christmas tree with tons of presents just waiting to be torn open. I never really took the time to think of what a help we could be to those less fortunate than we are—especially around the holiday season—until last year.

You see, the student council at my elementary school, Bookside Elementary, holds a fund-raiser every year to collect goods for the homeless. The four officers deliver the goods to Faith Mission in downtown Columbus. Because I was the school treasurer last year, I got to help deliver all the goods.

We had boxes filled with canned goods, gloves, mittens, scarves, and children's books. The three other officers and I taped up the boxes, loaded them, and went off to the Faith Mission. When we walked inside, it was so depressing—rooms full of homeless people, dressed in what were almost rags. They all looked so sad.

Knowing we had boxes full of goods to help their Christmas holiday be a little merrier was one of the greatest feelings I have ever had. Yeah, we were upset that we had to miss our class holiday party to deliver these goods, but to tell you the truth, if I had the chance to do it again, I definitely would. It made me appreciate my Christmas dinner and all the gifts a little more. Heck, I appreciated my house even more. But the best part was receiving a letter weeks later telling us what a help our fund-raiser was to them.

This year, instead of thinking of what I want to get, I will be thinking of what I want to give.

FUND-RAISERS

Starting Small

Megan Martel Jackson, age 13

LAST YEAR, THREE OTHER STUDENT COUNCIL OFFICERS AND I had the idea to hold a canned-food drive and a mitten tree for our main fund-raiser of the year.

It started out really small. We talked to the other student council representatives about our idea, and they really liked it. At our next meeting, we made posters to hang up around the school so the students would be informed of what was going on. We also made announcements over the public-address system.

At first, the student council was bringing in cans, but the rest of the school wasn't very motivated. So we held another meeting to see what we could come up with. We thought of finding some way of showing each class how much they were helping. In the front hall at school we put up dividers, one for each class. On each divider was a long piece of graph paper with a box on the floor at the bottom. When students brought in cans, representatives put them in the appropriate boxes and tallied the results by class.

This got the school motivated. We were bringing in so many cans! Our mitten tree got so full that we had to start putting the gloves and mittens under the tree. When it came time for the fund-raiser to end, we packed up the cans and brought them down to Faith Mission. We had so many boxes of cans and mittens that we had to borrow a van because they wouldn't fit into a car!

The Faith Mission thanked us for our donation. Our project made everyone in the school feel like they really made a difference. It started out small, but turned into something pretty big.

A Walk That Helped the World

....

Kirsten Marie Berg, age 12

I MADE THE WORLD A BETTER PLACE TO LIVE BY WALKING FOR the American Diabetes Association (ADA).

It all started on a sunny Saturday morning around 7:45 A.M. I got up, got dressed, and my neighbor dropped my friends and me off at school. Once everyone arrived, we got in the instructor's car and headed for St. Paul. There we signed in our group. Since we had earned so much money for ADA, we all got T-shirts. We put them on and started walking. The walk was around Como Lake.

We walked for awhile and had fun doing it. When we got hungry, we stopped for fresh apples and bagels that ADA supplied. The walk was supposed to be a six-mile walk, but we only got to walk four-and-a-half miles because we got there late. Still, we got tired but kept walking for the cause. It felt great to be helping the ADA.

I am proud to say I raised $70 myself, and our school raised almost $1,000. Only about thirty people participated in all. I feel great knowing I helped the world out!

The Good in Us

Chelsie Monkiewicz, age 12; and Julia M. Ryan, age 12

THIS YEAR, AS SEVENTH GRADERS, WE DECIDED TO TAKE PART IN community service. When we received the list of after-school activities, we thought it would be a fun thing to do in our spare time.

Mr. Hough, the teacher, expected only ten to twenty kids. He was amazed when he had received about sixty permission slips, and more were coming. We thought it would be fun working with Mr. Hough, but we weren't prepared for how it would make us feel inside.

Our first activity took place in October. We were going to be having a Haunted House for grades kindergarten through four. The purpose was to raise money and bring in food for the local food pantry. We thought we would raise about $50, get between two and three pounds of food, and have about 250 people show up. We were amazed to find that we had raised about $150, collected six pounds of food, and had more than 600 people show up. We were not only successful in raising money and getting food, we put smiles on people's faces, and we had a blast. In fact, as some people were leaving, they said, "I can't wait to see what next year is going to be like." Neither could we.

Our second activity lasted from the end of November to mid-December. We were planning to have a dance, but not a regular dance. We were going to have people dance for two hours with one fifteen-minute break. After the success of our Haunted House, we couldn't wait. In order to participate, each person had to collect at least $10 in pledges. As the week went on, we noticed that almost everybody was collecting more than the minimum. Maybe it was the holiday spirit, or maybe it was just knowing that some people don't even have a Christmas—either way, it felt good inside.

Again, we exceeded our goal. We raised approximately $1,400 and were able to not only purchase toys for the less fortunate children in our community, but also provide a Christmas dinner for each of their families.

In time, our community service group plans to assist people in our district who need help with the chores of daily life. We're going to help with things like yard work, housework, and shopping.

We are really glad we took part in community service. It taught us that we should help the needy and disabled as well as the average person. And, it taught us that community service should be taken more seriously. The most important thing we learned is that looking good on the outside is definitely not as important as feeling good on the inside.

Penny Wars

....

Leslie Chen, age 14

THIS BEING THE FIRST YEAR I HAVE BEEN AT TROY HIGH School, I was surprised at the things the student government and various clubs do to get the whole student body to participate in helping people less fortunate.

In November, our student government held "Penny Wars," where students would bring in pennies and drop them in containers provided in every fourth-hour class. It was fun. You could "bomb" other classes by putting coins or dollars into their containers. For example, if you put a quarter in another classroom's container, twenty-five cents worth of pennies would be taken from their total. So it was possible for a class to have a negative number. Only the pennies counted for your class; everything else counted against you.

Every afternoon, members of student government would count the pennies to see which classes were in the lead, write the totals on a chart posted in the hallway, and announce the top classes during the next morning's announcements. The top three classes got a pizza party. Penny Wars lasted only a week, but we raised about $9,000. Our goal was only $8,000. The money was donated to a student our age who had cancer, to help pay for his medical bills. A story about our school and Penny Wars was even shown on the news of a local TV station!

In December, one club held a food and clothes drive. This time, we brought in clothes, toiletry items, canned foods, and other things to be donated to local people who were in need of them. The items were collected in each first-hour class. This time, the top three classes got a doughnut party and were recognized during the announcements the next day. The drive wasn't as fun as Penny Wars, because you couldn't bomb other classes, but the school was able to collect more than enough items.

It's great that the staff, student government, and clubs at Troy High have taken so much time and energy to organize these events. They got the whole student body to take part and help others less fortunate, in a fun way. They also made me realize how lucky I am that my parents can provide me with food, clothes, and everything else I need—really, more than I need.

I think other schools should try to organize fun events like Penny Wars to help the poor, too. It's the least you can do to help, and you can actually have a really fun time doing it! You will be surprised by the number of people who will want to join in and help. And remember, that one little thing you do can help make the world a better place for someone else.

Climb for a Cure

Grant F. Gartland, age 12

THE CLIMB FOR A CURE IS WHERE PEOPLE GET TOGETHER AND climb all fifty stories of the IDS Tower in Minneapolis (that's 1,280 stairs, to be exact). The reason I did this was not to win a prize, but to raise money for a good cause.

The Climb is an event to help raise funds to find a cure for Cystic Fibrosis. Before the Climb, kids between the ages of seven and eighteen went out and asked people to sponsor them. Most sponsors gave a $5 to $10 flat pledge. Others pledged per floor/story. Usually, these sponsors pledged from $.03 to $.15.

Well, the first thing I did was find out more about the Climb for a Cure. I wrote to the companies who were sponsoring this event at the Climb for a Cure headquarters. They sent me a registration sheet to fill out before I could get my pledge sheet and go out and get pledges. I got the sheet, filled it out, and sent it back. After I was all signed up to do the Climb for a Cure, I went out to get pledges. This year was the first year I had ever done it—I think I collected over $100 worth of pledges for the Cystic Fibrosis Foundation.

I wanted to learn more about Cystic Fibrosis, so I looked it up in the encyclopedia. Here is what I found: Cystic Fibrosis has two main symptoms—an enormous appetite for food, and a persistent cough that doesn't clear the throat of thick sticky mucus. Although there is no cure for the disease, some patients have been helped by a diet high in protein and calories but low in fats. It also helps patients to be hit in the back once a day to loosen up the mucus.

Finally, the day of the Climb arrived. Registration started at 8:00 A.M. At 8:30 A.M., the race climbers started climbing. (A race climber is someone who races everybody else and tries to get to the top first.) Then at 9:00 A.M. all the fun climbers started to go up. Fun climbers are people like me who do it for the heck of it or for the satisfaction of knowing that they are pitching in to help the world.

Amazingly, the Climb for a Cure goes fast for such a long distance—only fifteen to twenty minutes! At the top of the Climb for a Cure is "The Survivors Party." At the party, there are free Subway sandwiches, free T-shirts, and the KDWB "Dave Ryan in the Morning Show." It was all there. You could get autographs and win free T-shirts and cool prizes! There was only one problem—the whole thing had to end and everybody had to go home.

I got a feeling of accomplishment from doing the Climb for a Cure, because I was one of a small group of people who devoted their time to go out and do something for the community. I walked away knowing I did something good. (We didn't actually walk away—we got to ride the elevators down to the bottom.)

Alcohol, Tobacco, and Other Drugs

Just Say No

....

Bjorn M. Neuville, age 8

THE WORLD WOULD BE A BETTER PLACE IF NO ONE SMOKED.

My grandma got cancer and she is in the hospital. She came home, but then she went back. We can't see her now, so never smoke. I will never smoke or take drugs or chew tobacco or drink alcohol.

In Loving Memory
Babette Olson
May 17, 1998

If Only Kids Didn't Smoke

....

Jesse Berger, age 8

ONCE I SAW THESE TWELVE-YEAR-OLDS AND THEY WERE SMOKing. One of them wanted me to smoke, and I said "NO! You guys are too young!" I went home and told my mom and dad. They went down to talk to them. The world would be a better place if kids would not smoke.

A Pledge

Jessica M. Levitan, age 8

I WANT TO HELP MAKE THE WORLD A BETTER PLACE. I WANT TO help people and help the world. When I grow up, I want to be a doctor to help people who are sick or who take drugs. I will pick up garbage and care for the trees. I will love the world.

Just Don't Do It

....

Margaret Berg, age 18

I'VE ALWAYS BEEN INTERESTED IN BUSINESS AND MANAGEMENT, so during my junior year of high school, I enrolled in marketing. Students in marketing can join a club called DECA. DECA members have an opportunity to use the information they learn in class at competitions later in the year. I decided to join, just to see what it was all about. It was in that competition that I helped to make the world a little bit better.

For the competition, my friends, Jeanette and Jason, and I decided to focus on communicating the hazards of tobacco and marijuana. Jeanette had lost a grandparent to lung cancer, I had just kicked the habit myself, and Jason had always been emphatically against smoking anything. Thus, our group was formed. We had to devise a business plan, put the plan into action, and write a ten- to forty-page manual telling the outcome of the project.

The theme we came up with was Just Don't Do It. We asked the Nebraska governor, Ben Nelson, to designate the week of December 2, 1996, Just Don't Do It Week. We then approached the American Lung Association, the American Cancer Society, P.R.I.D.E. Omaha, and the University of Nebraska Medical Center to line up speakers during our week. Their topics covered the effects of tobacco advertising on teenagers' perceptions of smoking, the side effects of smoking cigarettes and marijuana, and the costs of both. I was asked by the American Cancer Society to speak at the Great American Smokeout press conference about why I quit smoking and the methods I used.

To promote our campaign, we posted a billboard on the corner of a major intersection in Bellevue, placed flyers and posters in strategic locations around the school, and ran announcements on the daily bulletin. We even pasted almost 5,000 flyers on Pizza Hut pizza boxes. It took hours. We also created a web site containing information about our project. It got at least fifty hits per day.

Jason and I spoke at Mission Middle School about tobacco advertising and the physical effects of smoking. Every child at the presentation signed a pledge sheet promising never to smoke. Soon after, the three of us produced a commercial in conjunction with TCI Cable of the Midlands to promote our project and let the community know of our plans to educate Bellevue about cigarettes and marijuana.

Jeanette and Jason hired an acting group to discourage tobacco use among elementary school kids. They performed a play about Octapuff, an octopus who begins to smoke. The other fish in the sea tell him how unhealthy it is and finally convince him to quit.

When our Just Don't Do It week arrived, we wondered if it would be a success. We needn't have worried. Every speaker attracted at least two hundred students—a bigger turnout than any of us had anticipated. We had at least one speaker every day, and sometimes two! The American Lung Association donated an information booth so students, faculty, and visitors could view and gather flyers, brochures, and pamphlets.

Finally, the state convention. Each project group interviewed with two judges. The judges asked questions about our project, such as what its strengths and weaknesses were, and what we wished we had done differently. The next day, the top three winners in each category were announced. When the announcers got to the public relations category, we held our breath. "The first-place winner is . . . (drumroll) . . . Bellevue West!" The West DECA kids erupted in a shower of screams, yells, hoots, and hollers, while Jeanette, Jason, and I ran up to the stage.

Since we were among the top three winners in the public relations category, we qualified for the national competition in Anaheim, California, where our project placed among the top sixteen public relations projects in the nation.

Though we were not the first-, second-, or third-place winners at the national convention, Jeanette, Jason, and I were pleased with our project. We were determined to inform the city of Bellevue about the hazards of smoking cigarettes and marijuana, and we achieved that goal.

THE LARGER WORLD

Moving Mountains

Christine Davis, age 14

MY OPPORTUNITY TO HELP MAKE THE WORLD A BETTER PLACE
came on Saturday, March 14, at 2:45 P.M., when my brothers and
I spent eight hours working as volunteers for the Mission: Moving Mountains' banquet to benefit missionaries in Africa.

Our task was to prepare thirty tables for the three hundred
guests expected. Each table seated from eight to ten people. My
older brother, John, placed butter on the tables. Paul, my little
brother, and I poured ranch and Italian dressing into little
bowls for each table. Then, three other girls and I placed six different kinds of bread into wicker baskets. When the ice arrived
in huge bags, the boys put the ice into individual glasses.

As the guests arrived, bidding on silent auction items began.
There were many different items for the bidding. They ranged in
size from a watercolor set to a desk chair. Laughing and talking
among themselves, the guests seemed to be enjoying this part of
the banquet. The guests quickly devoured the hors d'oeuvres—
beef jerky, barbecued elk meatball, venison sausage, different
kinds of cheese, and crackers.

The final preparation started at 6:30 P.M. We put the salads,
desserts, coffee, and water pitchers on each table. The servers,
one wearing a tall white chef's cap, started to set up the food.
There was a vast variety of food: chili made from wild elk, barbecued venison meatballs, shepherd's pie made with elk and vegetables, venison roast and gravy, wild goose stroganoff, moose meat

The Larger World   119

pie, silver and red salmon, wild boar pork loins, black angus beef, smoked trout, wild rice casserole, and creamed potatoes.

As more and more people arrived, we had a mad rush to accommodate all the guests. We ran out of table space, silverware, coffeepots, and pitchers. One of the workers had to borrow silverware from another church. As waiters, we carefully watched for ways to serve the guests. We offered more bread, coffee, or water, and when the guests finished eating we collected dirty dishes.

After the door prizes were gone, a professional auctioneer began to auction off more expensive items, including a boat trip for six, a luncheon for four, a first-time flight lesson, a painting, and a weekend for two. The auctioneer was making jokes and talking very fast.

Following the auction, as guest speakers talked about some of the goals of Mission: Moving Mountains, I felt good knowing I had helped this organization make the world a better place for others. Mission: Moving Mountains improves the lifestyle of thousands of Africans in poor villages each year.

Working in a Moscow Orphanage

....

Timothy W. Wood, age 15

IT WAS HARD LEAVING MY FAMILY AND FRIENDS BACK IN AMERica to work in a run-down orphanage, but I have enjoyed every bit of this cultural exchange experience. And, I think I helped to make another part of the world a better place.

Three years ago, when I was twelve, my family and I moved to Moscow, Russia. We were invited by the Moscow Department of Education to work with orphans and juvenile delinquents, taking care of them and schooling them at home—in this case, in our apartment.

An orphanage during communist times, the orphanage we work with fell into disrepair after Perastroika. When we first visited the building, it looked like a bomb had been dropped inside. The outside shell was all that remained. My father and I played a major part in remodeling the building grounds. We also did other jobs, such as demolition, construction, and filling trenches. We would work all day, six days a week, to make sure the buildings looked presentable for the inspectors. My dad and another man were in charge of building cabinets, bookcases, vanities, doors, and anything else out of wood. In just one month, my dad and I had built and installed fifty-two vanities, with sinks and mirrors, in the dormitory rooms of one building. Other families worked on other construction projects. Now, when I return to America, I will be able to do all sorts of jobs.

Once the construction and remodeling was done, I became an orphan leader. One of my duties is to make sure the child I am in charge of stays within the guidelines set for this orphanage. I have to admit, it is hard to train orphans who have lived on the streets all of their lives. Their view of right and wrong is a whole lot different than ours. How do you teach a child not to steal when that is all he has been taught to do? Nevertheless, our work has not been in vain.

I have also had to learn to speak Russian. Overall, it's pretty similar to English, especially technical terms such as "computer" and "radio." As in most languages, the hardest part is learning the grammar. I am still struggling with elementary Russian grammar. Luckily, the six orphan boys we work with have all been to America for at least one summer, so they all know English.

Occasionally, I go out to different orphanages and schools with other students to teach them about character. Being a chalk artist, I have an easy way to get children's undivided attention. When children are disruptive, I begin to draw and tell a story that goes with my picture. They usually settle down right away, listening with open ears and closed mouths.

I am studying to become a musician and artist. Here in Russia they have special schools for certain subjects. For example, they have separate schools for music, sports, art, and other vocational abilities. A Russian student will attend a regular academic school for about six to eight hours a day, then he or she will head for the specialty school for another six hours or more. Even though I am studying vocational subjects, I do not attend Russian schools, because my parents have decided to school me at home.

My time in Moscow has changed my life, and I hope it has changed the lives of the orphans I work with.

Small Acts

....

Amanda Dewey, age 12

EACH INDIVIDUAL PERSON CAN HELP MAKE OUR WORLD A PEACE-ful and better place. One way we can do that is by bringing people from different races and cultures together.

My family has done that more than once. For starters, they adopted me from South Korea when I was five months old. More recently, my family and I home-stayed two soccer players from Slovakia. They came here for the USA Cup soccer tournament. It was a chance for them to learn about life in the United States, and we learned a little bit about their culture.

Bringing our community together is another way to make this world a better place. In school, our class made thoughtful cards for the family of a girl who died in a car accident. I know it meant a lot to them, because Jamie's family sent us a card back saying how special our cards were because they were homemade and came from the heart.

I try to extend my help to animals, too, because the environment is a very important part of our world and we need to take care of it. A mother duck on our pond rejected two baby ducks. They would have died without her care. My mom and I called the Department of Natural Resources, which took care of those ducklings until they were ready to live on their own.

It says in the Bible to love your neighbor as yourself. If every person around the world would do that, each act of love would come together to make a big difference.

Without Food

....

Eric Kreiner, age 12

From February 27 to February 28, I participated in a thirty-hour fast. I collected $110.50 in pledges from family and friends to be donated to Brother De Paul's mission to Haiti. This money was used to buy food for the students who went to the school that the mission had built in the Haitian slums. For about half of the children who received this food, it was their only meal of the day. They usually only get beans and rice, and some of the children only eat half of their food and bring the rest home to their family.

During that thirty-hour fast, I received absolutely no food—only water and juice. The event was organized by the youth group at Epiphany Catholic Church in Coon Rapids. My own youth group supplied food for a big party at the end of the thirty-hour fast.

I learned from my experience that the poor people of Haiti suffer a lot! Thirty hours of fasting isn't that long compared to what the people in Haiti go through. Some of them go two to three days without food. At the end of the fast, I couldn't wait for the poor children of Haiti to receive the food from the school. I discovered that it only takes a little effort to give a whole lot to others.

COMMUNITY PRIDE

The Storm of '97

Dan Hawkins, age 12

I'LL NEVER FORGET THE STORM OF 1997. IT WAS TUESDAY, JULY 1, early evening. Not only did we lose our power, but our backyard was a total mess. But our backyard was nothing compared to the rest of the neighborhood.

My family and I went outside after the storm had cleared. Trees were down—some on top of wires—garages were flattened, and shingles had been blown off roofs. I thought to myself, "What a mess! It's going to take forever to clean this up."

The next day, cleanup started. First I helped with my own backyard. Next I headed down to the neighbors' house. I helped as much as I could to clean up their mess, carrying branches and tree stumps up a hill and to the boulevard. Believe me, it was not easy work. The neighbors were really appreciative and it made me feel good that I could help out.

Everywhere you looked people were helping other people. It made me proud to see everyone pitching in and working together. Work got done a lot faster because everybody lent a helping hand. That's what a community is all about.

Welcome to Milan

Laura Molden, age 13

MY NAME IS LAURA MOLDEN. I AM THIRTEEN YEARS OLD AND an eighth grader at Lac Qui Parle Valley School. I live on a farm with my mom, dad, and sister. I belong to the Milan Challenger's 4-H Club, which is the organization I wish to tell you about.

Milan is a small town in West-Central Minnesota well known for its fishing and goose hunting. During the year, we get a lot of out-of-town visitors, so it's important that we keep our community looking good so we can be proud of where we come from.

This past year, our 4-H Club took on a very important project for our town. We wanted to make a lasting impression and create a pleasing atmosphere for people who drive by or stop in our town.

At the edge of town is Milan Lions Park. A number of years ago, in front of the bathrooms there was a privacy wall with rose-maling on it. Some vandals spray painted the sign with black graffiti, and it looked really bad. My sister, Michelle, had the idea to clean up the park and repaint the privacy wall and picnic benches to make the park more pleasing to the eye. You see, the park is at the edge of town and is one of the first things visitors see as they drive into town.

Now, this was kind of a touchy subject, because when she had wanted to clean up the park in the past, a 4-H family member who was also part of the Lions Club did not feel it was an appropriate community pride project. It was the Lions Club's responsibility to take care of the park. Still, Michelle felt that sprucing up the park would really make a difference in its appearance.

When she brought it up the following year, the idea was agreed upon. We needed to get permission from the Lions Club, but they were more than happy to let us do the work.

Now our great adventure started. The bathrooms were really dirty and needed paint badly. One of the Lions Club members had a high-pressure washer and helped us wash down the bathrooms and prepare the wood for painting.

The privacy wall outside the bathrooms also needed several coats of paint to cover up all the black graffiti. Because the privacy wall looked so plain after it was painted white, we asked the Lions Club if we could put "Welcome to Milan" on the wall. They were more than happy to let us do that and also said we should put our name somewhere for all the hard work we did.

Our club does not have very many older members. Most are between the ages of three and eighteen, with the majority being in elementary school. There was a job for everyone, though, regardless of age.

We had a lot of fun doing this project. It was a lot of work scraping and painting the tables and the bathrooms, but when you work together for a common goal, you can really have fun and feel proud of the job you did. It was especially great working with younger children and setting a good example of leadership and community pride. What was most rewarding? When we were all done, you could see the pride in everyone's face. And the park looked great!

Travelers along Highway 7 can now enjoy the Milan Lions Park a little bit more since we helped spruce it up. This park is used for overnight camping during hunting and fishing season, as well as by people who need to stop over and take a rest. A cash donation of $100 was given to the City of Milan from a hunter from the Twin Cities because he was so impressed with how the park looked. When we heard this, we were even prouder of our accomplishment.

Our motto at 4-H is To Make the Best Better. It is our hope that, regardless of age and ability, and no matter how big or small the project, by working toward a common goal we can learn to work together and have fun along the way. By doing this, we can make the world a better place.

K Kids Kare

....

K Kids, grades 3-5

IT ISN'T EVERY DAY THAT A GROUP OF TWELVE STUDENTS CAN make a difference in the world around us. However, our group has helped to make our community and our world a better place to live.

Our group is called K Kids. You might know about the Key Club in high schools. We're like the Key Club, only an elementary version. We have a president, vice president, treasurer, and secretary. Our teacher, Ms. Chovich, helps us come up with ideas and keeps us on track. We also have one class representative from each of our third-grade, fourth-grade, and fifth-grade classrooms.

Our school, Frontier Elementary, is the newest of three elementary schools in our community. We live in Payson, Arizona, a town about two hours north of Phoenix and one and a half hours south of Flagstaff. Our town is a rural community of about 11,000 people. We have one middle school and one high school.

Our group thought that a book drive would be a wonderful way to help build our new school's library. Last year, our group collected over one-thousand books. This year, we ran another book drive for our library and have collected another five-hundred books to date.

In our community, we have a Time Out Shelter, a place where abused women and children can avoid domestic violence. When women and children go to this shelter, they have usually had to leave their homes quickly and haven't been able to take a lot of things with them. We wondered what we could do to help these families and decided to sponsor a coat drive. We asked families to donate any coats they might have. Our local paper, *The Roundup*, even put a picture of us on their front page announcing our coat drive. K Kids collected 122 coats, of all sizes, for the Time Out Shelter. Needy families in our community also came to our school during the coat drive saying they heard about our project and could not afford to buy coats for their children. These families were able to find coats for their children in the boxes we had in our room. We felt very proud and helpful.

To help the environment, we collected pennies last year to help save the rain forests. We placed jars in each of our classrooms to collect pennies. We collected enough to adopt two acres of the Belize Rain Forest. This was a great project that helped all of us realize the importance of trees and wildlife.

Our local nursing home has allowed us to adopt them. Last year, we sang songs for the residents and made them Easter baskets. Our group has made posters to decorate their walls, and on Valentine's Day we delivered handmade valentines to each resident. We want the people there to feel loved and not forgotten.

In January of this year, we collected and delivered over 150 stuffed animals to our local emergency room. We put up posters at school asking students to bring in any stuffed animals they no longer wanted. One kindergartner brought in over fifteen animals! He dragged a huge bag in all by himself and gave each stuffed animal to us with a big smile on his face. We donated all the stuffed animals to the hospital so that injured children who come to the emergency room could have a cuddly animal. We thought these stuffed animals could help hurt children feel less frightened.

Just recently our teacher heard about a project to collect school supplies for students in war-torn Bosnia. The project, called Shoe Box Filled With Hope, was organized by a military man stationed in Bosnia. He asked teachers and schools to collect all the pens, pencils, markers, and school things they could. He said the schools had been rebuilt since the war but the students had no school supplies. So we placed a shoebox in each classroom and asked students to donate pencils, markers, scissors, erasers, and so on. When we combined the classes' donations, we filled eight large shoeboxes with these supplies. That's a lot of school stuff.

During our last meeting, we decided to hold a couple of bake sales and send the money we earn to a Florida organization to adopt an endangered manatee. Each $20 that we make will allow us to adopt one manatee. We know that we will probably never see a manatee, since we live in the middle of Arizona, but we know that this money will help the Save the Manatee Club keep one or two of the remaining 2,600 manatees alive!

We think it is important to take part in making our world a better place to live!

Save Our Silverton

Lauren Elizabeth Cheney, age 10

CAN A FEW KIDS MAKE A DIFFERENCE IN A SCHOOL DISTRICT? Can you influence or change a decision that adults have made? The answer is yes, even if you're only ten years old.

My school district, in Everett, Washington, has an environmental camp in the woods. It's called Camp Silverton and has been running for fifty years. A week before school got out last spring, my friend Sarah and I heard that the district was going to close the camp forever because it needed lots of repairs, totaling $250,000! Sarah and I didn't think it was fair that the camp was closing just before we got to be fifth graders. It's a tradition for fifth graders to go there, nearly 3,000 kids go every year. But what could we do? And in only a week?

We thought we should show the school board that kids really care about the camp. To get money, we organized a penny drive at our school. In three days, we collected forty-seven pounds of pennies, $252 in all. That was the start of the S.O.S., Save Our Silverton, fund. Our contribution got the attention of the town newspaper, and a reporter came to write a story about us. When it was published, another school decided they would help, too. Grownups also asked how they could help. We found out that lots of people loved their memories of going to camp.

The school board was amazed by all the people who wanted to keep the camp open. They decided to give the S.O.S. committee two months to raise the money. After school was out, Sarah and I made our own S.O.S. committee. The adults who were involved had some great ideas and did things that were too hard for us kids to do, but we were able to design and sell S.O.S. T-shirts (the governor has two of them), make S.O.S. buttons to sell, decorate donation jars and put them at grocery stores, make signs, get a donation from the Lions Club, hold an S.O.S. fund-raiser at a baseball game, get letters to the editor published, and hold two car washes. In all, we donated about one-hundred hours of our time.

By the August school-board meeting, we had raised $170,000. The board decided it was enough to keep the camp open for us fifth graders, but it couldn't promise anything for next year's kids.

This is how it ended up: From the start of that school year, enough people heard about S.O.S. to bring the fund up to $230,000, while several companies donated things that the camp needed. Camp Silverton is now saved for the future!

You might think I did all this work for myself, to get to go on the camping trip with my class. But actually, I had been to the camp many times before. My family rented it every summer, so I wouldn't have missed out, really. But I wanted to save it for others. I think it's a great place. I wanted others to have as much fun there as I did. Some Everett kids would never get to camp in the woods if it weren't for Camp Silverton.

Sarah and I made a pole with all the kids' names on it who helped. We put it at the camp to remind others that kids can make a difference and change things for the better.

Kids Can Make
a Difference

....

Joshua Jay Lenz, age 10

HI! MY NAME IS JOSHUA JAY LENZ. I AM TEN YEARS OLD AND IN the fourth grade. I would like to share with you some fun and rewarding community projects that my brother, cousins, friends, and I are involved in.

My Scout troop, part of Pack 460 in Tiltonsville, Ohio, had a food drive for two churches and a soup kitchen in our community. We collected about 850 items in all, which went to needy families. I was surprised at how many cans we collected.

My brother and I sent Saint Patrick's Day decorations, along with drawings to color, to patients at Children's Hospital in Columbus, Ohio. We hope the decorations and pictures helped to cheer up the children. We are now in the process of making drawings and Easter decorations to send to the children.

Another project my cousins and I are involved in is going to the nursing home. Every other week after school, we go to the nursing home to visit the residents. We were going to adopt one as our grandparent, but they were all so nice that we decided to adopt them all. Some of the residents don't have any family around, so they really look forward to our visits. We tell them about ourselves, and they tell us stories about themselves, their families, and their childhood. Their stories are always so interesting. And I know they like to hear our stories, too. We really enjoy visiting with them.

One of the lady residents was a sergeant in the Army. She has a picture of herself, which made the cover of a magazine, hanging on the wall in her room. Boy, was she pretty! She said she was a mean old girl in her younger days, but I find that hard to believe. She is one of the sweetest ladies there. Another lady resident likes to collect teddy bears. She has them all over her room. Some of them are from when she was a little girl. They are all in good shape.

One of the male residents is teaching us how to sing a song in Polish. He sings pretty well. He loved to sing and dance when he was younger. I bet he is still a good dancer. He is a lot of fun. We always visit him last, because we can't stop laughing when we see him. He makes the funniest faces and always likes to tell us funny stories and jokes. He really makes our day. Sometimes, we laugh all the way home.

We love the residents who live there; they are so much fun to be around. We made them decorations to hang in their rooms and on the big bulletin board in the hall. This way everyone can enjoy them. We are making them Easter decorations now, and plan to have an egg hunt, a sing-along, reading activities, and maybe even put on a play for them. The ideas are endless. I can't wait to see how well they like all the projects we have planned for them.

My brother, cousins, and I are also in the process of calling homeless shelters and battered women's centers to see if they need blankets, books, toys, or anything else for the children who stay there.

Helping others is a lot of fun, and very rewarding. I would like to encourage other kids to do the same. There is nothing like the feeling you get when you see a smile on someone's face and know that you are the one who put it there.

Our Panel of Judges

Professor Chester G. Anderson

A Wisconsin native, Professor Anderson is one of the world's leading scholars on the works of James Joyce. He has taught English at such prestigious schools as Columbia University and University of Helsinki in Finland. He has received numerous research grants and honors for his excellence in teaching, including the Ruth Christie Award for Excellence in Teaching (1994). Professor Anderson has edited and published numerous books and articles. He lives in Falcon Heights, Minnesota, and currently teaches at the University of Minnesota.

Mayor Sharon Sayles Belton

Mayor Sayles Belton began her public service as a teenager, volunteering at Mount Sinai Hospital in Minneapolis, Minnesota. While in college, she worked for civil rights, traveling to Jackson, Mississippi, to register voters. As the first African-American president of the Minneapolis City Council, and the first African-American and first female mayor of Minneapolis, Sayles Belton is a powerful role model. In 1997, Mayor Sayles Belton was elected to her second four-year term as mayor of Minneapolis.

John Burstein

A performer and creator of the popular children's character, Slim Goodbody, John Burstein has created many PBS television series, records, filmstrips, and videotapes. He is also the author of the Wonderful You children's series published by Fairview Press. John has been awarded the Parent's Choice Award and the Healthy American Fitness Leader Award from the President's

Council on Physical Fitness. Having founded and directed the International Kids Fitness Association, he is dedicated to improving fitness training and health education. John lives in New York City with his wife and teenage son.

MARLY CORNELL

Marly Cornell is a social justice activist, artist, and writer who has worked twenty-four years in health care. Her drawings and paintings have been commissioned by organizations such as Primarily Primates, CEASE, and the Animal Rights Coalition. She has written for various publications, including *The Animal's AGENDA,* where she served for several years as a contributing editor. Marly has traveled worldwide to speak at many universities about her work. Currently, she is the chair of the Ethics Committee for the Institute for Chemical Dependency Professionals at Fairview University Medical Center in Minneapolis. She is also a contributor to the Speakers Bureau of the Animal Rights Coalition, and a member of the advisory committee for Fairview Press. Marly lives in St. Louis Park, Minnesota.

LAURIE BETH FITZ

Laurie Beth Fitz is the Co-Executive Director of the Twin Cities American Cancer Society (ACS), Minnesota Division. She has been with ACS for thirteen years. In addition, Laurie teaches at the Acting Studio in Minneapolis and writes studio pieces for their performance workshops. Prior to her work at the American Cancer Society, Laurie produced a children's science television program for the Science Museum of Minnesota and was an instructor at the University of Minnesota in Speech/Communications. She serves on two national task forces for the American Cancer Society and has received recognition for her work in creative outreach and multicultural volunteer empowerment.

Senator Rod Grams

Senator Rod Grams (R-Minnesota) was sworn in as a member of the United States Senate on January 4, 1995. He serves on several Senate committees, and in 1996 he was appointed by President Clinton to serve as a Congressional Delegate to the 51st Session of the United Nations General Assembly. Prior to this governmental service, Senator Grams spent twenty-three years in the field of television and radio broadcasting.

Nkauj'lis Lyfoung

Nkauj'lis Lyfoung is currently the project coordinator for *Don't Believe the Hype* on Channel 2/17, Twin Cities Public Television. An actor, director, and playwright, Nkauj'lis is also the co-founder of Pom Siab Hmoob Theatre, the first professional Hmong theatre in the United States. Nkauj'lis serves on numerous panel discussions sponsored by Asian American Renaissance, Walker Art Center, and the University of Minnesota, and has been a representative at national conferences dealing with youth issues.

Patrice Snead

The Community Programs Coordinator for the Minnesota Historical Society, Patrice also serves as the chairperson of the 1998 Juneteenth Film Festival, a KFAI community radio programmer, and an active volunteer in the African-American community. She also designs, administers, and facilitates public programs of cultural and historical significance to the state of Minnesota, highlighting communities of color from various socioeconomic backgrounds in the Twin Cities Metro Area. Patrice lives in Minneapolis, Minnesota.